Nov. 95. HAPPY 40th BIRTHDAY
SORRY WE MISSED THE BASH
HOPE YOU ENJOY THIS BOOK
PAULINE B

SHORT WALK PUBS IN

The Yorkshire Dales

Nick Channer

COUNTRYSIDE BOOKS
NEWBURY, BERKSHIRE

First Published 1995
© Nick Channer 1995

All rights reserved. No reproduction
permitted without the prior permission
of the publishers:

COUNTRYSIDE BOOKS
3 Catherine Road
Newbury, Berkshire

ISBN 1 85306 374 6

Designed by Mon Mohan
Cover illustration by Colin Doggett
Maps by Douglas Cossar

Produced through MRM Associates Ltd., Reading
Typeset by Paragon Typesetters, Queensferry, Clwyd
Printed by Woolnough Bookbinding Ltd., Irthlingborough

Contents

Area map showing locations of the walks.

Publisher's Note

We hope that you obtain considerable enjoyment from this book; great care has been taken in its preparation. However, changes of landlord and actual closures are sadly not uncommon. Likewise, although at the time of publication all routes followed public rights of way or permitted paths, diversion orders can be made and permissions withdrawn.

We cannot of course be held responsible for such diversion orders and any inaccuracies in the text which result from these or any other changes to the routes, nor any damage which might result from walkers trespassing on private property. However, we are anxious that all details covering the walks and the pubs are kept up to date and would therefore welcome information from readers which would be relevant to future editions.

Introduction

To some, perhaps, the 680 square miles of the Yorkshire Dales National Park represent a harsh, upland landscape of bleak fells and lonely moorland. However, those who are well acquainted with this distinctive region of the country will tell you that it is a unique and magical part of Britain – truly a walker's paradise. Despite the unpredictable climate and the plunging temperatures of the Yorkshire winter, the Dales have a softness about them, a rare intimacy not generally found among the hills of Northern England. When people fall in love with the Yorkshire Dales, the affair usually lasts a lifetime.

One of the region's greatest assets is its immense variety of scenery. Wherever you venture in the Yorkshire Dales, majestic landscapes await you – dramatic sweeps of high moorland, undiscovered emerald green valleys, limestone scars, spectacular waterfalls and timeless villages of charming stone cottages and inns, where the culture and way of life have changed little over the years. The Dales, so lovingly portrayed in the books of James Herriot, are characterised by their rivers – the Wharfe, Ribble, Ure, Nidd and Swale among others – and here, too, the walker has the chance to stroll along peaceful paths beneath towering fells and crags.

The walks in this book have been devised to reflect the special beauty of the Yorkshire Dales. Many of the routes take you to the very heart of the region, discovering the hidden delights of remote Arkengarthdale, the broad sweep of spacious Wensleydale and the charming little villages of Swaledale. There is also the spectacular limestone country of the western Dales – the land of the Three Peaks. Perhaps here, more than anywhere else in the area, there is a true sense of space and freedom – it is a place of endless views and wild summits. Adventure country. Several walks coincide with stretches of the Pennine Way and Dales Way, two of Britain's most popular long distance trails.

The routes, which vary from 2¼ miles to 4 miles, are all circular and begin and end at a local inn. Most are straightforward and physically undemanding, though several walks

6

involve a little hill climbing and some brief stretches of open moorland. The pubs are all comfortable village hostelries where walkers and families are welcome and real ale is served. Food is available most days and is usually on offer from 12 noon until 2 pm or 2.30 pm and from between 6 pm and 7 pm until 9 pm or 9.30 pm (7 pm to 9 pm on Sunday). However, times do change so it is advisable to check beforehand. Hours of opening and other relevant details are included. Permission has been given for cars to be left at the inns whilst the walks are undertaken, but I would urge you to consult the landlord before setting out, just to be sure.

I also recommend you take a copy of the appropriate Ordnance Survey map, as well as some form of basic waterproof clothing – the weather in the Yorkshire Dales can be changeable and erratic. Remember, too, that temperatures can drop dramatically on the higher ground. A good pair of walking shoes or boots is also essential as the ground can become extremely wet and muddy in places.

I hope that the walks and the traditional inns described in this book help you to spend an enjoyable few hours in one of Britain's most beautiful National Parks – the magnificent playground of the Yorkshire Dales.

Finally, my thanks to Douglas Cossar for his invaluable help and assistance in the preparation of this book.

Nick Channer
Spring 1995

Arkengarthdale
The Charles Bathurst Hotel

1

From its source high on the moors the Arkle Beck flows down about 11 miles to join the Swale near Grinton. The valley it forms is Arkengarthdale, one of the most remote and lovely of the dales, up which a minor road makes it way, to cross the moors by the isolated inn at Tan Hill to Brough, and from which an old Roman road crosses the Stang Pass to Barnard Castle. In this quiet and charming valley, surrounded by wild countryside with long views, the remains of the lead mining industry are apparent at every turn, and a wealth of footpaths allow one to explore them at leisure.

It was in 1656 that Dr John Bathurst, physician to Oliver Cromwell, bought the valley, and he and his descendants played a major role in the development of the lead mining industry and in the life of the dale. His son and grandson were both called Charles Bathurst, and it was after them that the Charles Bathurst Hotel was named. Although renovated and modernised, the building goes back to the 17th century, and it provides a warm welcome to visitors exploring the dale.

The inn is open every day from 11 am to 11 pm, except on Sundays, when the normal licensing hours are kept. An extensive menu is available, including steaks, gammon, chilli, haddock, pizza and a selection of vegetarian dishes, and specialities are the steak and mushroom pie, the Yorkshire pudding and the Whitby seafood platter. There is a children's menu. The inn is a freehouse, and its usual real ales are Exhibition and Theakston XB. Families with children are welcome, as are well-behaved dogs, and the hotel also offers overnight accommodation.

Telephone: 01748 884265.

How to get there: The inn is situated on the minor road up Arkengarthdale, 3 miles from the B6270 Swaledale road in Reeth, west of Richmond.

Parking: The inn has its own car park.

Length of the walk: 3 miles. Map: OS Outdoor Leisure 30 Yorkshire Dales Northern and Central areas (inn GR 999031).

In medieval times Arkengarthdale, the most northerly dale within the National Park, was a hunting forest inhabited by deer, wolves and wild boar. Midway round, we come to the little Dales village of Langthwaite, which featured in the opening shots of the television series 'All Creatures Great and Small'.

The Walk

From the pub turn right and walk up the road for about 100 yards. Bear right just before a copse to take the waymarked bridle path for Fremington and Hurst. Follow the walled path and in front of you are glorious views of Arkengarthdale, its wooded slopes rising to meet the skyline. Descend the path, curving to the right beside the wall. Pass through a wooden gate and join a track on a bend. Continue ahead and on the right are views of Langthwaite church nestling in the dale.

Pass some cottages, cross a cattle grid and then go over the Arkle Beck, the soft, soothing sound of its rushing waters adding an extra dimension to the enjoyment of the walk.

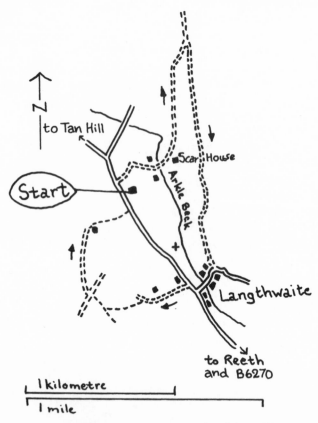

to Tan Hill

Start

Scar House

Arkle Beck

Langthwaite

to Reeth
and B6270

1 kilometre

1 mile

Continue along the drive into the grounds of Scar House, which
stands in a commanding position on the lower slopes of the
dale. Follow the drive towards the house and, just a few yards
before you reach it, bear sharp left to join a stony track. When
this swings right towards the house, continue ahead up the
slope through the trees.

Pass through a white gate and follow the track as it emerges
from the woodland to climb the grassy slopes of the dale. Keep
going along the walled track and soon you pass a bridleway on
the right. Make for a dilapidated gate in the next boundary and
continue to a pair of stone cottages. The views over Arkengarthdale are stunning at this point. Pass to the right of the cottages
and aim for some stone outbuildings and byres. Follow the

track to the right of them and after several yards you come to a gate. Do not go through it, but instead veer to the right and sweep round the open moorland pasture to make for a gate to the left of a ruined old byre. At this point you are beginning the return leg of this walk, recrossing the same boundary you negotiated by the cottages, only this time a little further up the slopes.

Join a muddy track running between walls. Soon you pass through another gate and along this stretch there are again superb views across Arkengarthdale. The Arkle Beck can also be spied snaking along the valley floor at the foot of the steep slope. However, moorland plantations soon restrict views of the beck and the encircling hills. Pass a bridle path to Hurst on the left. Through the curtain of trees on the right you can just make out Scar House, which we encountered earlier on the walk. Pass an old stone dwelling on the left and now the track narrows to a path. Follow it down to the woodland and walk between the trees. In autumn and winter there is often a deep carpet of leaves along here. The walls enclosing the path are thick with lichen.

The outline of Langthwaite church is soon seen again and on the left is a conveniently placed seat in memory of Kenneth Burley of Huddersfield. Keep the church in view on the right and note the buildings of Langthwaite clinging to the lower slopes of the dale. The Charles Bathurst Hotel, where this walk began, can be seen in the distance. Soon you reach the road on an S-bend. Turn right and walk into Langthwaite. Pass the Red Lion and the delightfully unspoilt village shop and continue over the bridge to the junction. Bear right, then first left by a green and some cottages. Follow the bridleway alongside the flowing gill and head towards some cottages. Pass between the farmhouse and its buildings and continue to a stone cottage. Just beyond it is a junction of tracks. Avoid the turning on the right and walk ahead up the slope.

After a few yards the track bends left. Leave it at this point and continue ahead on a grassy path. This part of the walk reflects Arkengarthdale's industrial past. Deep gulleys and long abandoned lead workings serve as ghostly reminders of the days in the mid 19th century when lead production here was at its height. Keep going until you see some vague tracks on the right,

Langthwaite in Arkengarthdale.

heading towards some mounds and relics of old spoil heaps. Bear right and follow the tracks, with the village now on your right.

Cross over at the road and follow the 'footpath only' sign. Walk along the track and at this point Scar House is seen once more. The track runs down to some cottages. Pass through the gate and then enter the field, keeping to the left of the cottages. Once in the field bear right and head down the dale.

Descend the slope, with some power lines on the right, and make for a wall down below you on the right. Head down to the school, keeping the wall on the right. Go through a gate by the school yard, walk along to a squeeze stile and then out to the road. Turn left and return to the inn.

② Reeth
The Black Bull

The village of Reeth, set round its large green, was once a thriving market town serving the farming and lead mining communities. Today, with its hotels and cafés and gift shops and its Swaledale Folk Museum, tourists are its main source of income and it is very busy on summer weekends.

The inn is open every day from 11.30 am to 11 pm (Sundays 12 noon to 3 pm and 7 pm to 10.30 pm). An extensive menu is available, including lasagne, chilli, curry, cod, haddock and scampi, and there is always a special dish of the day. Other specialities include home-made pies and Old Peculier casserole. The inn is a freehouse, and real ales served include Theakston Bitter, XB and Old Peculier and Tetley's. Families with children will feel at home here, and well-behaved dogs are also welcome.

Telephone: 01748 884213.

How to get there: The inn is situated in the centre of Reeth, which is on the B6270 road through Swaledale.

Parking: Park round the village green (honesty box).

Length of the walk: 3½ miles. Map: OS Outdoor Leisure 30 Yorkshire Dales Northern & Central areas (inn GR 038992).

Field paths with pleasant views over Swaledale are followed by a long stretch of attractive riverside walking.

The Walk
Leave the Black Bull and turn left. Walk along to the road junction, cross over the main road and bear right along the narrow road which passes the bus shelter, the telephone kiosk and the Burgoyne Hotel. Drop slightly at the end of the green and bear left along a 'No Through Road' which soon bears right again and descends. Where it turns left again at the bottom by Arkle House fork right off it down a stony track, and soon you have Arkle Beck to your left. Follow the beckside path until you pass under a stone road bridge and bear right up to the road. Turn right over the bridge and follow the road to the right, but just after this bend go through a signposted stile on the left and bear half-right across the field to a gated stile.

Follow the same direction across the next field to a wall corner. Go through the stile in the wall on the left and bear right up the slope, with the wall to your right. Go through another stile and follow the wall to a stile by a gate, then keep forward along the track to join a metalled road. Follow the road up through the hamlet of High Fremington and where it forks turn left uphill by End House. Already you will see a footpath signpost ahead – turn right at it along the narrow walled lane. When the lane turns right walk straight forward over a stile by a gate and follow the edge of the next field, with the wall to your left. At the end of the field go through the stile and walk straight across the next field. In the following field you have a wall to your right. There are pleasant views to the right over Swaledale. Pass through a gate and continue with the wall to your right. Cross a stile by a gate and bear left to follow the wall on your left. At the end of the field pass through the gap in the wall ahead and continue with the wall to your left. At a kink in this wall go through a gap-stile in front of you and keep your direction, but now with the wall on your right. When the wall

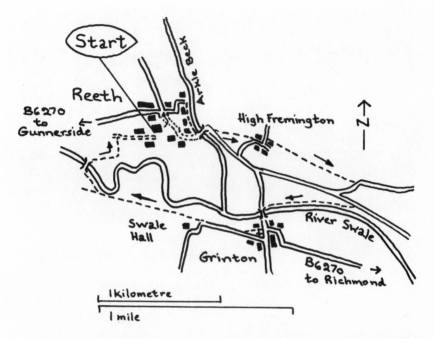

ends keep forward across the field, bearing very slightly left to a stile onto the next motor road.

Turn right down the road, and at the foot of the hill fork left along a minor road signposted to Marrick Priory. Walk downhill until you reach some trees, where you will see a stile on the right. Cross it and bear right along a clear path, with the Swale down on your left. Cross a stile and keep forward along the riverside path, which should be followed to Grinton Bridge. Turn left to cross the river by the bridge. Opposite the Bridge Inn take the gravel track on the right, which has Grinton church to the left and a very attractive old house to the right. At the end of the track keep forward along the footpath, with the river to your right. Soon some steps lead up to a stile onto a road.

Turn right along the road. Where it bends left and climbs to a large old house (Swale Hall) fork right off it along a walled lane signposted as a bridleway. After a while the Swale is down on your right again. Then the walled lane leads you away from the river once more under tall old trees. The walled lane ends at a gate, but the path continues by the wall on the left. Having

Morris Dancers at Reeth. (Yorkshire and Humberside Tourist Board)

crossed a gap-stile by a gate, the way ahead down the tree-lined old lane is blocked, and you must go through a gate on the left and then bear right along with the fence and old wall to your right. Go through the stile by the gate at the end of the field and keep forward with a fence to your left and the river close by on your right. Half-right you will see the suspension bridge over the Swale. Follow the river bank to it (notice the ancient cultivation terraces, or lynchets, on the far side of the river) then cross and turn right along the fenced path to a small gate. Keep forward across the next field on a clear path which bears slightly left, crosses a stile by a gate just before a straggly hedge, then continues forward to cross a small footbridge and bear left uphill to a gate into a walled lane. At the top of the hill turn right along the track. Ignore the footpath sign on the left beside the surgery, but at a road junction where there is a wooden foot-path sign turn left. After about 100 yards turn right along a tarmac lane, and where it turns left again keep straight forward along a ginnel. Where this ends keep forward for a few more yards before bearing left to return to your starting point.

Feetham
The Punchbowl Inn

Feetham and Low Row are two villages that stretch out alongside the main road up Swaledale and merge into one, with sloping greens in front of the houses. The main road used to be higher up the hillside, which gave Low Row its name, and we climb up to this older highway on our walk. Mining and knitting were once the main occupations of the inhabitants, and the tall, stone 17th-century Punchbowl used to be the Miners Arms. It is particularly popular with walking and cycling clubs.

The inn is open on weekdays from 11 am to 11 pm and on Sundays from 12 noon to 3 pm and 7 pm to 10.30 pm (and the tearoom next door all day every day). Among the dishes available are gammon, lasagne, chilli, stroganoff, Swaledale sausage, 'Hog Grill' and T-bone steak and the specialities include giant Yorkshire puddings with a variety of fillings and 12″ pizzas. On Saturdays soup and sandwiches are available all day. Real ales include Theakston Bitter, Mild, XB and Old Peculier, John Smith's Bitter and occasional guest beers, and the

17

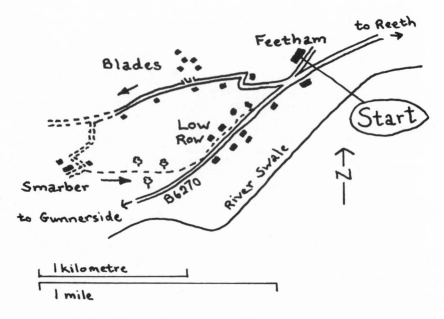

bar has 140 different brands of whisky! There is a beer garden at the rear and a patio at the front. Children are welcome and there is a family room. Dogs are accepted in the bar, but not in bedrooms. The inn has 16 rooms and also a bunkhouse annexe. Telephone: 01748 886233.

How to get there: The Punchbowl is set back from the B6270, the main road up Swaledale, in the hamlet of Low Row.

Parking: In addition to the pub car park there is parking by the roadside.

Length of the walk: 2¼ miles. Map: OS Outdoor Leisure 30 Yorkshire Dales Northern & Central areas (inn GR 986984).

A steep climb on a tarmac lane gives sweeping views of Swaledale. An upland hamlet is visited and several fine old farmhouses are passed. The return to the valley is on a green track.

18

The Walk

Leave the Punchbowl and turn right to slant down to the main road, but as soon as you reach it fork right off it again up another narrow tarmac road. Follow this steeply up, pausing frequently to enjoy the views, all the way to the top of the hill. When the gradient eases at Rose Cottage look right to see the small scattered hamlet of Blades, and it is worth making a detour to see the old cottages more closely. Having done this, return to the tarmac lane and continue along it.

Now the continuing ascent is gentle, past scattered farms and barns. When the tarmac ends, a double concrete track continues forward, soon bearing left downhill. Before it does, pause once more to enjoy the view, because this is the highest (and furthest) point of the walk. Follow the track down to the farms at Smarber. One of the houses, and only one, is on the left of the track, and immediately to the right of it is a metal gate. Leave the track, which curves right to the farms, go through this gate and find yourself on a clear, grassy track bearing left downhill. Soon Isles Bridge across the Swale comes into view down on the right with the wooded valley of Haverdale Beck beyond.

The tiny settlement of Blades.

19

The track passes through a gate into scrubby woodland. Keep following it downhill. When it fords a beck there is a bridge for pedestrians and a little waterfall. The track leads down to the main road in Low Row. Turn left along this, but in a few yards climb the grassy bank on the left to a bench and make your way along the grass parallel to the road. If you bear left up the slope to a house with white railings, you can join a track leading forward from it. This in turn joins a tarmac lane which leads down right past the Literary Institute and Assembly Room (and the telephone kiosk) to reach the main road by the Old School. Now there is no alternative to walking along the road until you come to the access road to the Punchbowl.

4 Muker
The Farmers Arms

In the 17th and 18th centuries, when the people of Muker earned their living by lead mining, the population was larger and there were three inns. Now there is only one, and sheep and cattle farming and tourism are the main sources of income. Knitting is an old tradition here, and this cottage industry has been revived, with fine quality hand-knitted Swaledale woollens on sale in the village. The centre of the village is the parish church of St Mary, and the grey stone cottages cluster around it.

The exact history of the old, whitewashed Farmers Arms is not known, but it is now a popular meeting place for the local community and attracts a large number of tourists. It is open on weekdays from 11 am to 3 pm and 6.30 pm to 11 pm (winter 7 pm to 11 pm) and on Sundays from 12 noon to 3 pm and 7 pm to 10.30 pm. The menu includes steaks, gammon, curries, lasagne, a selection of vegetarian dishes (for example, broccoli and cream cheese pie), a variety of fish dishes, omelettes and salads. Snacks such as soup, sandwiches, baps, toasties, burgers

A typical Dales view.

and jacket potatoes are also available, as are children's menus and smaller portions. The home-made steak pie is a speciality. Several real ales are kept, including Theakston Bitter, XB and Old Peculier and the Butterknowle Brewery Bitter from Bishop Auckland. The inn has a family room, but children are welcomed throughout (as are well-behaved dogs). In fine weather the patio in front of the pub is popular.
 Telephone: 01748 886297.

How to get there: The Farmers Arms is situated in the centre of Muker on the B6270, the main road up Swaledale.

Parking: There is no private car park, only a small space at the front of the inn, so patrons are advised to use the public car park about 200 yards away at the east end of the village.

Length of the walk: 3½ miles. Map: OS Outdoor Leisure 30 Yorkshire Dales Northern & Central areas (inn GR 911978).

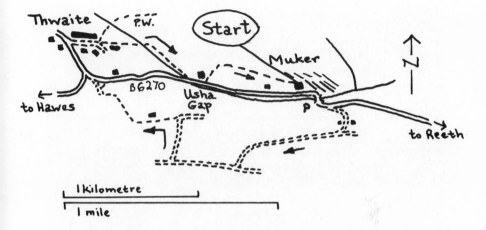

The outward leg is by a track which climbs gently to give fine views up and down Swaledale. A short detour can be made to a waterfall, there is a café at the halfway point and the return is by meadow paths with lots of stiles.

The Walk

Leave the Farmers Arms and turn left. Follow the main road to the east end of the village and cross the bridge. The entrance to the car park is on the right and the road bends left. In a few yards fork right off it up a signposted track which soon becomes a walled lane. After passing between two barns the track curves right and gently climbs the hillside. You pass an old limekiln on the left and there are fine views right to Muker and both up and down Swaledale. When you reach a T-junction with another walled track coming in from the left, bear right. A few yards after crossing a concrete bridge turn sharp right at another junction of tracks, down the hillside, still in a walled lane.

Where this lane turns sharp right by a small barn, leave it by going through a gate on the left and walking along with a wall to your right. Ford the beck and enter another section of walled lane. It leads past a barn. Having gone through a gate you have a wall only on the right and you pass an abandoned farm. Keep ahead on the track, with the wall to your right. Pass through another gate and still stay on the track near the wall on your right. Go through a gate in the wall corner ahead, and now the wall is to your left. The track soon bears slightly right away

23

from the wall, then turns left towards it again. Down on the right you will see a small wooden gate in the wall. Go through this and cross the beck by a footbridge to another gate. Either bear right down the track to the road and bear left along it or, if there has been recent rain and you would like to see an attractive waterfall, walk along by the wall/fence on the right to another small gate, descend the steps and bear left along a hollow way, then drop down the field to another small wooden gate and the road. Turn right towards the farm, then look right over the wall to see the waterfall. Now walk back along the road.

Ignore the road to Hawes on the left and continue to the hamlet of Thwaite. Notice the Victorian posting box on the left, then turn right in front of the Kearton Guest House (café). Where the lane curves slightly right fork left off it at a Pennine Way sign, through a gap-stile. Ignore the stile on the left signposted to Angram and keep forward along the clear path, with a wall on the left and a building on the right. Pass through two more gap-stiles and keep ahead in the direction of Muker, soon with the beck down on your right. Go through another gap-stile, now leaving the beck off to your right, and walk straight over the next field to another stile. Follow the wall on your left. Pass between a power line pole and a barn and walk forward to the next gap-stile.

The clear path leads ahead to a small wooden gate in the facing wall. Bear left over the old stone packhorse bridge and in a few yards cross a stile in the wall on the left. Turn right and keep the wall on your right to the next stile. Bear very slightly right across the next field to pass to the right of the barn, then bear left to another gated stile in the far wall. Now follow the wall on your left to the road. Turn left along it. Go through the entrance into Usha Gap Farm on the left, and opposite the right-hand end of the farmhouse go through the gap-stile on the right. A crowd of barking dogs welcomed me here, but they were all tied up! Turn left along the edge of the field, with a large barn to your left. Follow the wall along until on the other side of the field you will see a stile a few yards to the right of a gate. Cross this stile and follow the wall on your right. The path is now clear through a number of stiles and fields back to Muker. Almost immediately after reaching the houses fork right on a path downhill which returns you directly to the Farmers Arms.

Hardraw
The Green Dragon

5

The village of Hardraw is famous for its waterfall, Hardraw
Force, situated in the grounds of the pub, and for its brass band
contests which for many years have been held there in
September. The lands on this side of the Ure were owned in the
Middle Ages by Jervaulx Abbey, and the inn may well have
started life as a monastic farm or even brewery, because local
tradition has it that there has been an inn on this site for 700
years. With its roaring open fire in winter, the Green Dragon is
famous for its hospitable welcome, particularly to weary
walkers on the Pennine Way, which passes the front door.

The pub is open every day from 11 am to 11 pm (Sundays
12 noon to 3 pm and 7 pm to 10.30 pm, although soft drinks,
tea, and so on, are served all day). The menu runs from soups,
sandwiches, jacket potatoes and pies through salads, steaks,
chicken, gammon and scampi to a specials board, and meals can
be taken either in the bar or the dining room. There is a
children's menu and families with children, to whom the

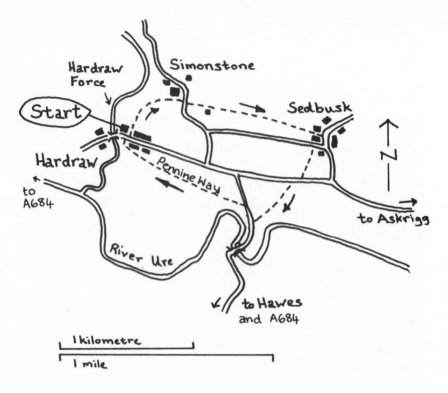

extensive grounds with the waterfall are particularly appealing, and well-behaved dogs are welcome. The inn is a freehouse, and Theakston Bitter, XB and Old Peculier are available on draught. There are 16 bedrooms, all en suite, including family bedrooms, and 6 self-catering apartments.
Telephone: 01969 667392.

How to get there: Hardraw is situated on the minor road along the north side of Wensleydale, west of Askrigg and almost directly opposite Hawes on the A684, from which it can also be reached by a minor road. The inn is in the village centre.

Parking: The inn only has a small car park for residents, but there is parking by the road in the village.

Length of the walk: 2½ miles. Map: OS Outdoor Leisure 30 Yorkshire Dales Northern & Central areas (inn GR 867913).

Typical paths through pastures, with lots of stiles, afford fine views over Wensleydale. The walk includes a short section of the Pennine Way. An additional attraction for this walk is the Wensleydale Creamery at nearby Hawes. The site includes a visitor centre and a viewing gallery, where you can see the hand-made, cloth-bound cheese in production.

The Walk
On leaving the Green Dragon turn left, then left again round the side of the building, but in a few yards there is a gate on the right into a paved yard (signposted 'Simonstone'). Cross this yard to the stile on the far side, then follow the paved path along the edge of the field, cross a stile, and continue on the clear path up the hillside towards a little house on the top. Steps at the top of the field lead to a stile. Pause here and look back over Wensleydale. Walk on up the next field, at first by steps, and just beyond the house and barn on the right there is a stile just to the right of a metal gate. Cross this and walk straight forward on the partly paved path across the next field to the stile on the far side, just to the right of a small barn. Now follow the wall on the left along, with the grounds of Simonstone Hall beyond, to a stile. With the entrance to the Hall to your left, turn right along the access drive to the next road.

Turn left for a few yards to a gated stile on the right. Cross this and bear right along a concrete farm track. Pass to the left of the barns and follow the track forward to a gate with a ladder-stile just to the left of it. Walk straight across the next field to pass to the left of a barn, then go through a stile by a gateway. Continue straight across the field to the stile. Keep on over the next field to another stile, and over the following one to a stile to the right of a barn. Go straight across the next field, bearing slightly right when you reach the barn, round a wall on the left to a stile. Continue straight ahead to the next stile, with the hamlet of Sedbusk now visible ahead, and then on the same line through several more fields and stiles to pass between houses to another stile and the village green in Sedbusk.

Turn right down the road, but a few yards past the old Primitive Methodist chapel, now a private house, with a Victorian pillar box ahead, turn right along a narrow road. Shortly after passing a gap-stile on the right (signposted 'Simonstone'), cross a gated stile on the left (signposted

27

Hardraw Force. (Yorkshire and Humberside Tourist Board)

'Haylands Bridge') and follow the waymarked path, which bears slightly right from the stile, steeply downhill, passing to the right of a barn, to a ladder-stile at the bottom. Walk straight over the field to the stile. The clear path now bears slightly right over the next field, before dropping to a stile by a line of tall trees onto the road. Cross diagonally right to the stile opposite. A very clear path bears slightly right down the next field towards the river and a bridge, crossing a slab bridge on the way. The path leads to a stile in the wall at the bottom of the field. Look ahead to see the huge meander which the Ure makes at this point. The church tower in Hawes is prominent beyond. From the stile keep straight forward down to cross an old stone-cobbled bridge with an ugly wooden rail. Walk straight over the next field to a stile onto the road.

Turn right and follow the road as it crosses a bridge and climbs through a low wooded escarpment. Immediately beyond this go up a few steps and cross the stile on the left (you are now on the Pennine Way). Walk along with the wall and wood to your left, and follow the clear path all the way back to Hardraw. As you approach the hamlet, the flagged path leads over a stone slab bridge across a beck coming from a farm on the right and continues forward to cross a farm track and reach a kissing-gate in the wall ahead. Now follow the wall on the right, soon joining a track which leads back to the main road opposite the Green Dragon.

⑥ Askrigg
The King's Arms

Askrigg is a delightful Dales village with a long street of stone houses and cottages. It was put on the map by the BBC who used it in the filming of *All Creatures Great and Small*, based on the stories of the late James Herriot, the famous Scottish vet who, in middle age, became a best-selling author. Long before it achieved television fame, Askrigg was renowned as a centre for clockmaking. It was also the main market town in Upper Wensleydale, boasting two annual fairs, for which Queen Elizabeth granted a charter in the 16th century.

The King's Arms was originally built for John Pratt in 1760 to accommodate one of the most celebrated racing stables of the day. It became a coaching inn early in the 19th century and since then it has been established as one of Yorkshire's finest and most famous hostelries. Filming took place here, too, during the making of the television series – the back parlour became 'the Drovers Arms', a favourite haunt of James Herriot and his veterinary colleagues. For the real ale enthusiast there is

a choice of several beers on handpump, Dent Bitter, McEwan 80/- and Younger No 3. Lagers include Beck's and McEwan's. Guinness and Scrumpy Jack cider are also on offer. Bar snacks include the Doorstep Bloomer and Dalesman Lunch. In addition, you will find soup of the day, potted salmon, stir fried vegetables, steak and kidney pie, seafood pancake and wild mushrooms with tagliatelle. There is a specials board from which to choose, as well as a children's menu. Well behaved dogs are welcome. The King's Arms has a pleasant courtyard at the rear, a noted à la carte restaurant, known as the Clubroom, and the popular Silks Grill, which is adorned with colourful racing silks. The inn is open from 11 am to 3 pm and 6 pm to 11 pm on Monday to Saturday and from 12 noon to 3 pm and 7 pm to 10.30 pm on Sunday.
Telephone: 01969 650258.

How to get there: The King's Arms stands on the main road in the centre of Askrigg, close to the church. The road, which runs through Wensleydale, is just to the north of the parallel A684, west of Leyburn.

Parking: There is a car park at the inn, as well as on-street parking in Askrigg.

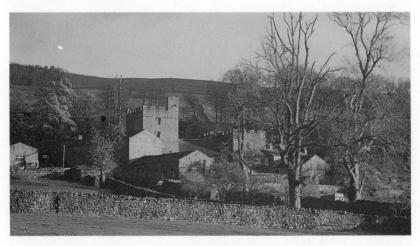

Nappa Hall.

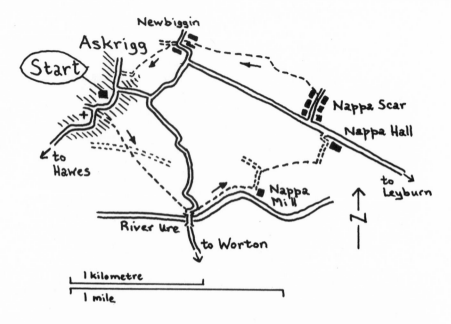

Length of the walk: 2¾ miles. Map: OS Outdoor Leisure 30 Yorkshire Dales Northern & Central areas (inn GR 948911).

The route crosses several low-lying pastures before following a riverside path towards a late medieval hall. Beyond the buildings of Newbiggin there are stunning views of Askrigg. Close to the start of the walk are two enchanting waterfalls – Mill Gill Force and Whitfield Gill Force.

The Walk

On leaving the King's Arms turn right and walk briefly along the main street, passing Skeldale House behind its railings on the left. The house doubled as James Herriot's surgery during the filming of *All Creatures Great and Small*. Immediately after Skeldale House, opposite the market cross, turn left along a tarmac lane (signposted to Worton and Aysgarth). When the lane opens out and forks, keep right and soon you will see a large gate in front of you. Pass through the gated stile just to the left of this and walk down the field, keeping close to the wall on your right. After a time the clear path bears left away from the wall, passes a derelict metal kissing-gate and drops onto the old Wensleydale railway line. Cross the line and turn left alongside it, but at another derelict metal kissing-gate bear half-right down the slope to a gap-stile in the wall below, a few yards to the right of a gateway. Descend a few steps and bear slightly left across the next field to the next stile. A paved path leads ahead over several fields (this section can be wet after rain) to the road by Worton Bridge.

Turn left along the road, but when it bends left cross the sign-posted stile on the right and walk along, with the river Ure on your right. Cross the footbridge and continue parallel to the river to a gap-stile in the next wall, just to the right of an old tree stump. Now bear half-left to the footbridge over a side beck, then walk straight over the field towards a large barn, where there is a stile just to the right of a large gate. Enter the yard at Nappa Mill and bear left up the farm access road. Just before the road bears left over a 'weak bridge' by a ford go through the gated stile straight ahead and bear half-right over the field to the gate in the far top corner. Go through this and follow the grassy track forward over the next field. Soon Nappa Hall comes into view up on the left. Leave the field by a gate on the far side and turn left up the track, passing to the left of the Hall.

Follow the track up to the road and turn left along it. Take the 'No Through Road' signposted to Nappa Scar and immediately beyond the stone farm buildings bear left for Newbiggin. The path now runs across a number of field boundaries before reaching a white gate. Pass alongside the front of Willow Garth, a pretty cottage, and walk to the little green at Newbiggin. There is a seat here. Cross the road on a bend and follow the track opposite. Pass over the Newbiggin Beck and then turn left immediately beyond the last stone building, before the track crosses open pastures. Head slightly right and make for the wide gap between stone walls. Veer right for a few yards to reach a gate and gap-stile. Cross into the next field and go across to the next boundary. At this point Askrigg looms into view below you, the village dwarfed by protective hills and fells.

Head down to the gap-stile in the next boundary, make for a gated stile and join a cinder track running to the road. Turn left and walk down to the junction by the Crown Inn. Go straight on and return to the King's Arms in the village centre.

⑦ Thoralby
The George Inn

Thoralby is a peaceful and attractive little village on the north side of Bishopdale, a side-valley of Wensleydale and one of the most beautiful of the dales. Lead and iron ore were once mined nearby, but now sheep and dairy farming and tourism are the main sources of income. The village used to have three inns, but the George is the only survivor. The present building dates from 1732, but tradition links the inn with the monks of Jervaulx Abbey. With open fireplaces and a modernised lounge and a very warm welcome, the George is at the heart of the village community.

The lunchtime opening hours are 12 noon to 2.30 pm (except Tuesdays in winter) with an 11.30 am start on Saturday. In the evening the pub is open from 6.30 pm (7 pm in winter) to 11 pm on Monday to Saturday, and from 7 pm to 10.30 pm on Sunday. The menu includes steak, gammon, chicken, lasagne, seafood, jacket potatoes and sandwiches, and there are vegetarian dishes. The steak and kidney pie is a speciality. A children's menu is also available. Three real ales are on offer, Black Sheep Bitter, John Smith's Bitter and Webster's Bitter. The inn has three rooms for overnight accommodation and those staying have been so impressed by the breakfast that they have been known to photograph it! Well-behaved dogs are welcome.

Telephone: 01969 663256.

How to get there: Thoralby is reached either by leaving the A684 Leyburn to Hawes road at Aysgarth or from the B6160 Bishopdale road; in each case the approach is by a narrow, hilly and twisty road. The inn is signposted in the village.

Parking: There are only a few spaces in front of the inn, but almost directly opposite a tarmac drive leads into a public car park.

Length of the walk: 3½ miles. Map: OS Outdoor Leisure 30 Yorkshire Dales Northern & Central areas (inn GR 999867).

A walk through meadows and pastures with good views of Bishopdale and Wensleydale. There are lots of stiles! At the halfway point is the village of Aysgarth, where refreshments (pub and café) are available. Nearby are the famous and spectacular Aysgarth Falls, best appreciated after a spell of heavy rain.

The Walk
On leaving the George turn right up the village street and follow it until you reach a fork. Turn right here uphill, in 40 yards passing through a gate (signpost to Aysgarth). A short distance further on ignore a track forking right through another gate. As you climb the view opens up over Bishopdale to your left. The track turns sharp right and in another 100 yards sharp left again. Leave it on this bend to go through the gate straight ahead and continue up another track (concrete where it passes through the gate) with a wall to your right. The track leads through a gate with a gated stile just to the left of it. Now bear right along the track, but after a few yards fork half-left off it, following the direction of the bridleway sign behind you, towards a marker post in the remains of an old wall ahead. Pass through the old

35

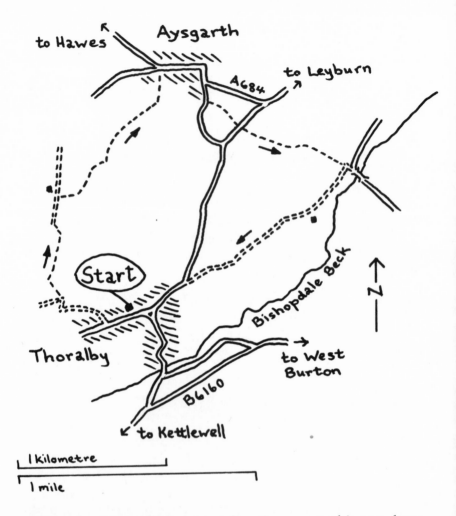

to Hawes

Aysgarth

to Leyburn

A684

Start

Bishopdale Beck

N

Thoralby

to West
Burton

B6160

to Kettlewell

| 1 Kilometre |
| 1 mile |

wall by the post and keep your direction across this very large field to a small gate in the far corner. Walk downhill with the wall to your right, but when you reach a gap in it, bear half left down to a gate in the wall at the bottom of the field which leads into a walled lane.

In a few yards you must ford a beck, but you can use the wall on the right. Walk up the walled lane, and as the slope eases you will see a building ahead (Folly House). Cross the signposted stile on the right a short distance before this building and walk along the field with the wall to your left. About 30 yards before the end of the field go through a signposted stile in this wall and bear half-right over the corner of the next field to the stile. Bear half-left over the next long field to a stile in the wall ahead just before the remains of an old wall crossing the field from the left. From this stile bear half-left again towards the right-hand end of a barn, crossing the beck by stepping-stones, and passing the barn to a stile by the gate a few yards to the right of it.

Bear very slightly right, cutting the corner of the field, to a gap in the wall ahead, and continue in the same direction to a stile on the far side of the next field. Walk pretty well straight across the following field to a stile just to the left of a power line pole, then follow the power lines over the next field to the stile. Keep by the wall on your left to the next stile and the next one, then bear slightly left to another one. Walk half-left over the next field to a stile by a large gate, then down the track, with a wall to your right and Wensleydale ahead. Cross another stile by a gate and keep on the track until it bears left. Here keep forward with the wall to your right, to a stile which leads into a short section of enclosed path which emerges through another stile onto a road.

Turn right through the village of Aysgarth. At the far end follow the main road right past the George and Dragon, but where it turns left again by the Aysgarth Garage, keep straight ahead on the minor road for 100 yards to a gap-stile in the wall on the left. Cross it and turn left along by the wall, but after about 40 yards bear slightly right to a gated stile in the wall ahead. Bear half-right over the next field to the stile, and walk straight across the following one (Bishopdale appears ahead) to a stile onto a minor road.

Go left for a few yards, then cross the stile on the right (signposted 'Eshington Bridge') and, ignoring the barn and the gateway beside it straight ahead, bear half-left down the field to a stile near the far left-hand corner. Now bear half-left to cross a broken fence, then walk down the shallow valley ahead, bearing right with it to a stile in the wall at the bottom. From this, walk forward, at first with a wall to your left, but where this wall turns left keep straight forward and at the top of the rise bear slightly left to a stile in the wall on the left. Now bear half-right to the next stile just to the right of a gateway, and from

Aysgarth Falls. (Yorkshire and Humberside Tourist Board)

it half-left past a wall corner, then drop diagonally down the field to go through a gap in the wall on the left near the bottom left-hand corner. Turn right downhill with the wall to your right, pass through the gate in the fence to the right of the barn and continue straight downhill (quite steeply) to a gap-stile in the facing wall at the bottom. Continue forward with the wall to your right and Eshington Bridge ahead to a stile leading onto Eastfield Lane.

Turn right along the narrow tarmac lane. We are now in Bishopdale, with Bishopdale Beck over to our left. Follow the lane almost all the way back to Thoralby. When you reach the main road turn left along it, and at the village green fork right to return to the George.

8 West Witton
The Fox and Hounds

West Witton lies on the south side of Wensleydale under the shadow of Penhill, which rises to 1,727 ft and on the summit of which a beacon used to be lit in times of danger. On the high ground to the east the racehorses from the stables in Middleham are trained, and a short distance to the west are the scant remains of a chapel of the Knights Templars. The houses of the village, once largely occupied by craftsmen and lead and coal miners who worked on the hills between Wensleydale and Swaledale, line both sides of a long village street. Each year on 24th August the Village Feast is held, ending with the 'Burning of the Bartle', a human effigy carried through the village.

The Fox and Hounds, perhaps the oldest house in the village, built around 1400 as a rest house for the monks of nearby Jervaulx Abbey, is open every day from 12 noon to 3 pm and 7 pm to 11 pm (10.30 pm on Sundays). There are open log fires in winter in both the bar and the dining-room. As well as sandwiches and a good range of hot dishes, including steaks,

39

gammon and several 'sizzling platters', the pub is justly proud of its specialities, a variety of home-made pizzas and steak and kidney pie. The landlord is keen to respond to the wishes of his customers and asks groups to ring up in advance to discuss the menus of their choice. A freehouse, the real ales include John Smith's and Webster's Bitter.

Telephone: 01969 23650.

How to get there: West Witton is on the A684 Leyburn to Hawes road, 4 miles west of Leyburn. The inn is in the village centre, on the south side of the main road.

Parking: The inn has a large car park.

Length of the walk: 4 miles. Map: OS Outdoor Leisure 30 Yorkshire Dales Northern & Central areas (inn GR 061883).

From West Witton the walk heads west along the lower slopes of Wensleydale to the site of the chapel of the Knights Templars. The return leg offers fine views across to Bolton Castle where Mary, Queen of Scots was imprisoned in 1568.

The Walk
From the inn turn left and walk along to the Wensleydale Heifer, a famous inn frequented for many years by James Herriot and his wife. Pass Old School Close and a milepost for Leyburn and Hawes. Follow the road as it curves to the right, beside a creeper-clad house called Wynbury on the left. Continue to the end of the garden and then bear left at the waymarker post for 'Knights Templars' church' (1 ½ miles). From this point there are very good views over Wensleydale. Cross the field to a squeeze stile in the far boundary. Continue for about 50 yards in the next field and then bear right at another squeeze stile. Turn immediately left and head for the field corner. Cross a stile and then skirt the edge of Mesnes Plantation. In the next field veer half-right, pass beneath some power lines and look for a galvanised gate just before the field corner.

Go straight across the field to the next squeeze stile. The main road can be seen from here, running between lines of trees on its way from West Witton to neighbouring West Burton. A

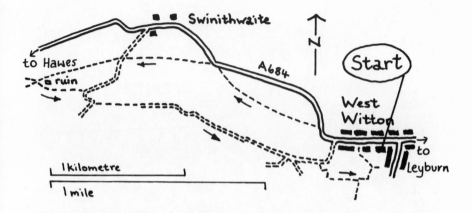

splendid view of Wensleydale dominates the scene. Head diagonally right in the next field and look for a gateway by the road. Near the gate is a footpath sign. Keep just inside the field, with the road beyond the boundary. Cross the next step stile and continue along the field edge. There are good views of Swinithwaite Hall down to the right. Go across a gated stile and continue, with the wall on the right. Cross a firm lane and keep going in the same direction until you reach the ruins of the chapel that once belonged to a preceptory of the Knights Templars.

Head diagonally left now and follow the sign for 'Nossill Lane via Langthwaite Lane'. Make for the slopes on the far side of the field and take the track running up beside the woodland. Pass through a gate and walk ahead until you reach the hard surface of a concrete farm lane. Turn right to follow the lane and as it curves right, go straight on up the slope, following the signpost.

From the higher ground a broad expanse of Wensleydale is clearly seen. The splendid outline of 14th-century Bolton Castle – impressively floodlit at night – is visible on this stretch of the walk. It is claimed that Mary, Queen of Scots escaped from the castle but dropped her shawl near Leyburn whilst fleeing and was recaptured within two hours. Look for a gate and footpath sign and walk ahead alongside the wall until you reach Langthwaite Lane, an ancient walled track. Follow the lane and

Remains of the Knights Templars church.

soon the buildings of West Witton come into view ahead. Eventually you join the road at the entrance to Chantry Park. Continue ahead down the lane and just before it bends left by some cottages, swing half-right up the bank towards Moorbank.

Follow the steps up through the trees and soon you reach a kissing-gate. Walk through the caravan park and follow the path, lined by fences, between the caravans. Go down the slope to cross a little beck, then turn left. The top of a waterfall is visible over to the left by the trees. Head straight across the field to a gated stile and veer half-left to a gap-stile. Make for the next gap-stile and then descend the wooded bank (signposted 'Village and Grassgill Lane'). Follow it down to the corner of the wall, pass through a gap-stile and then head down the field towards the houses of West Witton. At a footpath sign swing obliquely left towards the village. Make for a gap-stile in the field corner and head across to the corner of the next field, where you join a walled path. After a few yards you emerge at the front of the Wensleydale Heifer. Turn right to the inn.

Middlesmoor
The Crown Hotel

Middlesmoor, at the head of Upper Nidderdale, is regarded as one of the most spectacularly situated villages in the Yorkshire Dales. It stands on a breezy 900 ft hilltop, a delightful collection of stone cottages and winding streets, and from many vantage points – particularly in the vicinity of the church, rebuilt in the 1860s – there are superb views of the dale stretching towards Gouthwaite Reservoir. The population of the village has declined dramatically over the years, but there is still a true sense of community here. The Crown Hotel and the neighbouring general stores remain the focal points of Middlesmoor, which often becomes extremely busy during the summer months.

The Crown is very much a traditional village hostelry and also offers overnight accommodation. Dating back to the 18th century, the inn has a bar and separate dining room, both of which attract plenty of Dales hikers. Families are also welcome and food is served whenever the bar is open. The menu

Nidderdale. (Yorkshire and Humberside Tourist Board)

includes a range of meals – for example, lasagne verdi, pork sausages with Cumberland sauce, steak pie, and chicken, ham and leek pie. There are vegetarian dishes, sandwiches, ploughman's lunches and jacket potatoes. The Crown also has a specials board and a traditional roast on Sunday. Theakston Best Bitter and Younger are available on handpump and you will find Guinness, Scrumpy Jack cider, and McEwan's and Beck's lagers. Dogs are welcome and outside is a small play area for children. During the winter the inn is open from 12 noon to 3 pm and 7 pm to 11 pm on Monday to Saturday (closed Monday and Wednesday lunchtimes) and in the summer from

11 am to 5.30 pm (most days) and 7 pm to 11 pm. On Sunday the hours are 12 noon to 3 pm and 7 pm to 10.30 pm. Telephone: 01423 755204.

How to get there: Middlesmoor is reached from Pateley Bridge, which lies on the B6265 between Ripon and Skipton. The village is north-west of Lofthouse and you will find the inn on the left.

Parking: The Crown has a car park. Alternatively, there is a small public car park further up the village street, on the right.

Length of the walk: 2½ miles. Map: OS Outdoor Leisure 30 Yorkshire Dales Northern & Central areas (inn GR 092742).

The walk follows field paths down to the outskirts of Lofthouse, then makes for How Stean Gorge, a renowned local beauty spot. From here the route is across lowland pastures, at times following the Nidderdale Way. Apart from the obvious delights of Nidderdale, there are also two reservoirs, Gouthwaite and Scar House, which are worth visiting, if time allows, after the walk.

The Walk

From the inn turn right and then bear left just beyond the telephone box. Make for the church and then swing to the right of it to join the paved path between walls. Follow the steps down the hillside and head for a squeeze stile into the next field. Keep the wall on your left. Ahead of you is a breathtaking view of Nidderdale with the smooth expanse of Gouthwaite Reservoir glimpsed in the distance. Pass through a gate and walk down into the yard at Halfway House. There is a memorable view from here back to Middlesmoor and its delightful hilltop setting.

Pass between the farm buildings and look for a small gate in front of you. Head down the field slope, keeping close to its right edge. Look for a footpath sign down near the bottom right-hand corner of the field and make for a squeeze stile in the wall. Keep going with the wall on your immediate right. Ahead of you the road snakes through the dale. Make for the bottom boundary of the field and look for another stile not far from the

45

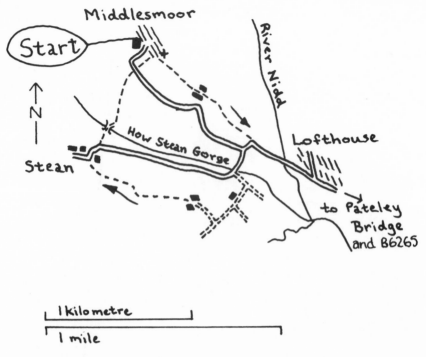

I kilometre

I mile

corner. Cross the next pasture – there is a byre over on the left here. Make for the road and turn right.

After about 50 yards the road bends right. At this point go straight on towards Stean Gorge. Follow the lane between walls and soon it swings right. A little further on you are treated to a charming view of the beck and the rock-strewn gorge through which it flows. Once over the beck turn left towards Ramsgill. After about 70 yards veer right, heading away from the water. Pass some farm buildings and then bear right at the sign for the Nidderdale Way. Pass some stone houses and cottages and a turning on the left to Ramsgill. Continue ahead, with good views across the dale, until you reach a rundown cottage on the right.

Pass through a gate on the right, immediately beyond the building, and follow a track across the fields. Head for Whitbeck Farm, keeping the boundary wall on the right. Just before you reach the house, look for a little gate to the right of it. Walk round the side of the house, then swing left towards some sheds and outbuildings. Pass through a waymarked gate on the right and head down to the beck. The footbridge has white railings. Cross the beck and then bear right. Keep the gulley on the right and walk to the corner of the field where there are some byres. Make for the gap-stile and head across the pasture, with the wall on your right. Cross a little beck, then head towards some farm buildings. Go through a gate, across a track and then pass to the right of the farmhouse. Follow the path alongside a beck, cross the bridge and turn right at the road. This is the hamlet of Stean. Pass Beckside Cottage and follow the road as it bends sharp left, then right by a red telephone box. After a few yards you reach a footpath to Middlesmoor on the left – part of the Nidderdale Way. Take the path and follow it through a small plantation.

Cross How Stean Gorge at a scenic spot – here the dark, peaty water runs beneath cold, dank walls like a subterranean stream. At the top of a flight of steps veer half-right and make for the next boundary. Bear immediately left and cross the following boundary, keeping the wall and fence on your left. At the road bear left and return to Middlesmoor, passing the old Wesleyan chapel built in the 1890s and converted to a private residence in the 1980s.

⑩ Foster Beck near Pateley Bridge
The Watermill Inn

Foster Beck is situated about a mile to the north of Pateley Bridge, Nidderdale's largest community. The town lies just outside the National Park boundary, though its fine position on the banks of the Nidd surely warrants inclusion. In summer its long, steep main street and attractive riverside paths bring many visitors to Pateley Bridge.

The Watermill Inn is one of the area's most famous and historic inns. It also boasts the unusual distinction of having been a working flax mill until about 30 years ago, and the adjacent 36 ft water wheel is one of only a precious few still surviving. The wheel, which has been restored to full working order, attracts many customers and sightseers throughout the year.

Inside the inn you will find a spacious lounge bar, pool room, dining-room and snug. Marston's Pedigree, Morland Old Speckled Hen and Theakston Old Peculier, XB and Best Bitter are on handpump. For the lager drinker there is a choice of

McEwan's, Beck's and Carlsberg. Guinness is also available, and there are three brands of cider – Woodpecker, Strongbow and Scrumpy Jack. Food is served every day and among the starters and snacks are soup, pâté, prawn cocktail and Yorkshire puddings. A selection of hot and cold sandwiches are on offer, and for something more substantial you could choose home-made steak pie, lasagne, chilli con carne, curry, lamb chops, mixed grill, sirloin steak, scampi or fish pie, among other dishes. There are also jacket potatoes, salads and platters, a children's menu, a daily specials board and a traditional Sunday roast. Families are welcome and there is a play area for children in the beer garden. The Watermill Inn also has eight en suite bedrooms. The pub is open all day throughout the year – from 11 am to 11 pm.
Telephone: 01423 711484.

How to get there: From Harrogate follow the B6165 to Pateley Bridge, which lies on the B6265 between Ripon and Skipton.

The Nidderdale landscape. (John R Fawcett)

49

Take the road west of the Nidd towards Lofthouse and Middlesmoor. The inn will be found on the left after about 1 mile.

Parking: There is a spacious car park at the inn.

Length of the walk: 3½ miles. Map: OS Landranger 99 Northallerton, Ripon and surrounding area (inn GR 147664).

This very attractive walk crosses the slopes of Nidderdale to reach the outskirts of Pateley Bridge. From the town the route back to the inn is partly along a riverside path adjacent to the river Nidd. Nearby is Gouthwaite Reservoir, a famous local attraction.

The Walk
From the inn go out to the road, bear left and then first left for Heathfield. After about 100 yards veer left (signposted 'Heathfield Caravan Park'). Follow the lane beside the beck and soon you are walking alongside rows of caravans. Pass a turning to Spring House and then take the next track on the left. Cross the beck, go through a gate and then curve to the right. At the top of the slope bear left and follow a muddy walled track. Further on, draw level with a cottage on the opposite bank of the beck and then take the footbridge over the water.

Continue on the walled track and, further up, there are very good views over the slopes of Nidderdale. Pass through a gate and continue alongside the wall. Go through another gate and head diagonally across the field. Make for the gate in the next boundary and then follow a grassy track with the wall on your right. Cross a field boundary and follow the path up the bank. On the higher ground there are far-reaching views over to the rooftops of Pateley Bridge and beyond. The path curves to the right to a gate. Pass through the gate and continue alongside the hedgeline. In the field corner go through several more gates and out to the road.

Bear left and walk down the lane towards Pateley Bridge. After about 200 yards, as the road begins to curve to the right beneath the boughs of some trees, veer obliquely left to join a path cutting alongside a wall. After several yards pass into the field on the left. Turn immediately right, keeping the fence and

50

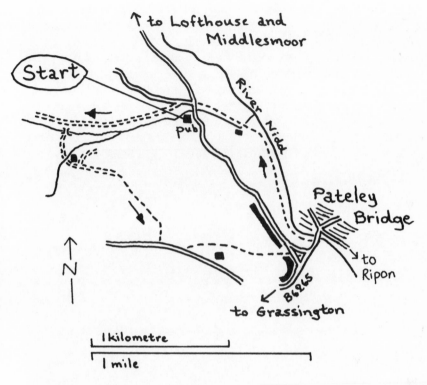

to Lofthouse and Middlesmoor

Start

River Nidd

pub

Pateley Bridge

to Ripon

to Grassington

B6265

N

1 kilometre

1 mile

hedgeline beside you. Head for the buildings of Pateley Bridge. The frontage of Eagle Hall is visible on the right. Make for the field corner and negotiate a gated stile. Keep going alongside the wall and fence, heading down the field slope. At length you reach a gate in the bottom right-hand corner. Beyond it follow a grassy track down to Pateley Bridge. At the road turn right for several yards, then left to follow a tarmac path between walls. Note the stone plaque on the left in memory of various local families.

At the main road turn left and pass Nidderdale Motors. Cross Low Wath Road and continue as far as the bridge over the Nidd. The little town of Pateley Bridge is laid out in front of you now. The bridge here was originally a ford or recognised crossing place used by monks from Fountains Abbey. Turn left and follow the path (signposted 'Corn Close'). The Nidd is on your immediate right. Pass the war memorial on your left, as well as

51

the recreation ground and sports field. Pass a spectacular weir and caravan park. Continue ahead on a raised path along the river bank. At length you pass through another gate and, about 50 yards beyond it, you can spot the vague outline of the path swinging diagonally left across the field. Make for the far corner, pass through another gate and walk along the banks of the beck to a high footbridge.

Beyond the bridge bear left and in a few minutes you come to a gate. Cross the next field to a galvanised gate and go out to the road. Bear left and return to the inn.

Starbotton ⓫
The Fox and Hounds

Starbotton, a limestone village in Upper Wharfedale, is very popular with walkers and trippers, the quaint old 17th-century cottages and nearby packhorse routes making it an obvious choice for a holiday or a day out. The village does not have a church, and the old Methodist chapel became a holiday home a few years ago. Starbotton achieved a degree of fame in 1686, when a terrible flood swept away many of the houses in the village.

The Fox and Hounds, one of the oldest buildings, was built as a private house. It is understood to have become an inn around the middle of the 19th century. Today much of its trade comes from the summer influx of tourists. During the winter months, however, it is much quieter. Then, a warming fire adds a welcoming, homely touch to the proceedings. In the bar, with its solid furniture and flagstones, you can sample a pint of Theakston Best, XB or Old Peculier. For the lager enthusiast there is McEwan's Export. You will discover a strong emphasis on vegetarian meals. Among the dishes are almond risotto, spicy butterbean crumble and parsnip and chestnut crumble. Other possibilities are chicken and leek crumble, home-made soup and Moroccan lamb. More traditional fare includes ploughman's lunches and home-made French sticks. There is also a children's menu and a daily specials board. Families are welcome. During the winter the pub is open from 11.30 am to 3 pm and 6.30 pm to 11 pm between Tuesday and Saturday (closed all day Monday between October and March) and from 12 noon to 3 pm and 7 pm to 10.30 pm on Sunday. In summer the hours tend to be the same apart from Monday when the inn is open between 11.30 am and 3 pm. No dogs please. One double and one single bedroom are available for a longer stay.

Telephone: 01756 760269.

How to get there: From Skipton head north on the B6265, then join the B6160 at Threshfield and follow the signs for Kettlewell. Starbotton is 2 miles further north. The inn is on the right. From Leyburn head west through Wensleydale and then turn left, just before Aysgarth, onto the B6160. Follow the road to Starbotton and the inn is on the left.

Parking: The Fox and Hounds has a small car park. Please notify the landlord before parking here to embark on the walk. If the inn is very busy, it may be easier to begin the circuit at neighbouring Kettlewell where there is a public car park.

Length of the walk: 4 miles. Map: OS Outdoor Leisure 30 Yorkshire Dales Northern & Central areas (inn GR 953748).

From the Fox and Hounds the walk heads south, following ancient packhorse paths and tracks along the lower slopes of Wharfedale. At Kettlewell it crosses the river and returns to Starbotton on a stretch of the Dales Way, upstream by the meandering Wharfe.

The Walk
From the inn turn left and follow the main road. Pass the telephone box and take the second left turning. After a few steps bear right and look for a gate on the left where a sign advises you to keep dogs on a lead. Follow the path as it curves

to the left after a few yards, then veer right towards the boundary wall. Beyond the next boundary wall turn left and go up the slope to a gated stile. Bear right and head south along the lower slopes of Wharfedale, following the contours of the valley. Pass a waymarker and continue. Cross the next boundary wall and keep going in a southerly direction. This part of the walk offers magnificent views across Wharfedale, a splendid patchwork of pastures, trees and soaring green fells. The river and the return leg of the walk are also clearly visible far below you.

Keep to the path, a dark, unmistakable scar, as it crosses a number of crumbling boundary walls. Pass beneath the boughs of some trees. The path bends left and then right. Cross a ladder-stile and continue along the slopes. Make for another ladder-stile and pass under some power lines. Soon you reach a third ladder-stile. Keep on the path, wet and muddy at times and, in places, uneven. Head for another ladder-stile and now the buildings of Kettlewell edge into view down in the dale. Beyond another ladder-stile the path heads for some trees and a stile. Continue with a wall on your right, over another ladder-stile, and now the houses of Kettlewell are clearly visible below.

Wharfedale. (Yorkshire and Humberside Tourist Board)

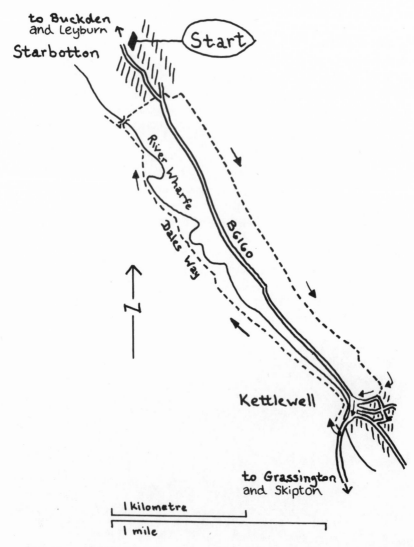

to Buckden and Leyburn

Starbotton

Start

River Wharfe

Dales Way

B6160

N

Kettlewell

to Grassington and Skipton

1 kilometre

1 mile

Descend the slope diagonally, passing under some more power lines. Cross yet another ladder-stile and head towards the village. There is a wall on your immediate right now. Soon the path curves to the right and runs down to a gated stile. Continue ahead into Kettlewell, joining a track running between houses.

At the road, on a bend, go straight ahead down to the main junction. Turn left and pass the large public car park. Take the road bridge over the Wharfe and bear right to join the Dales Way. Note the National Trust sign for Upper Wharfedale. Once past it, swing right (signposted 'Buckden' and 'Starbotton'). Descend the slope to follow the river bank. There are pretty views of Kettlewell on the opposite side of the Wharfe. Pass through a wooden kissing-gate and continue, maintaining the same direction, with the river on your right. In the field corner go through a gate and follow a concrete path parallel to the river. At times the path is very close to the water's edge, giving fine views of the rapids and swirling current. Further on the path, now wet and slippery in places, rises above the river. Go through a gate and follow a track, walled at intervals, as it crosses numerous field boundaries.

In a few minutes you come to a ladder-stile. Leave the wall at this point and follow the waymarker across this pasture towards some trees. Follow the path alongside a wall, cross another stile and then court the river bank once more. Head across an open pasture to another stile. Beside it is a National Trust sign for Upper Wharfedale. Continue ahead beside the river, cross a small footbridge and keep to the right of a wall. Make for several more stiles and a footbridge. The buildings of Starbotton can now be seen ahead. Cross a gated stile and go diagonally across the field towards a line of trees. Rejoin the river bank and soon you will come to a stile on the right. Cross it, then bear immediately left at a gap in the wall. Cross the next boundary and then turn right at the footbridge. The bridge was built with donations from the friends of the late Harry Smith, a lover of the Dales and a former chairman of the West Riding Ramblers' Association. Follow the walled track up into Starbotton. At the road turn left and return to the inn.

12 Hebden
The Clarendon Hotel

Hebden, east of Grassington, comprises rows of gritstone houses and cottages clinging to the west bank of Hebden Beck. The upper valley of this beck was once associated with the lead mining industry. Today, the village and the surrounding fells and moorland enjoy more peaceful times.

The Clarendon Hotel, in the centre of Hebden, is probably late Victorian and was built as a private house. In summer it is particularly popular with Dales walkers and those touring this part of Yorkshire. The interior of the hotel, which welcomes families, consists of a dining area and lounge bar, where the choice of real ales includes Tetley Bitter and Timothy Taylor Best Bitter. There is also Castlemaine XXXX and Lowenbrau for the lager drinker, as well as Guinness and Scrumpy Jack cider. The menu offers several starters, and among the main courses are Dales mixed grill, sirloin steak, fillet steak, chicken breast and breaded scampi. Bar snacks include sausage, steak sandwich, haddock, plaice, chicken curry and Yorkshire pudding.

There are various vegetarian dishes, salads, sweets and a children's menu. Food is available every day. The bar is open from 11.45 am to 3 pm and 6 pm to 11 pm on Monday to Saturday, and 12 noon to 3 pm and 7 pm to 10.30 pm on Sunday. No dogs please. The hotel can also provide overnight accommodation with en suite facilities.
Telephone: 01756 752446.

How to get there: The pub is situated on the B6265 Pateley Bridge to Grassington road. Hebden is about 8 miles from Pateley Bridge.

Parking: There is a car park at the inn.

Length of the walk: 3 miles. Map: OS Outdoor Leisure 10 Yorkshire Dales Southern area (inn GR 024631).

A streamside descent to the river Wharfe and a delightful stretch of riverside path are followed by a return over a series of stiles through pastures and meadows.

Scene in the Yorkshire Dales.

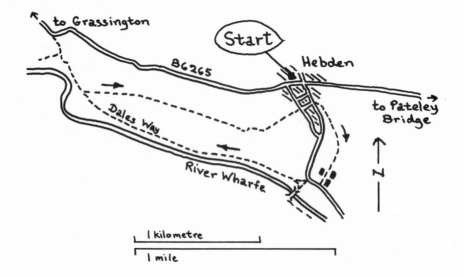

The Walk

On emerging from the inn turn left down the main road to the crossroads and turn right along the road signposted to Burnsall. Shortly after passing the old school on the left go through a kissing-gate (signposted 'Suspension Bridge') and follow the cobbled path towards the valley of Hebden Beck. Ignore a footbridge over the beck and keep forward to a gated stile in the wall ahead. Walk on parallel to the beck, soon bearing slightly right to a kissing-gate. The path now crosses the beck by a footbridge and follows the wall on the left (over it there is a fish farm), and where the wall ends keeps forward to cross a side beck by a little stone bridge, then a gravel track. You are walking on grass parallel to a track to your left towards a signpost.

Your direction is still towards the suspension bridge. To the right of the path is a fence, with more fish tanks beyond. The clear path leads to a drive between houses, then to a road. Turn right over the bridge and follow the road as far as the next signposted gate on the left. Our way now leads half-right over the field (signposted Grassington Bridge), but it is worth making a detour to test the springiness of the suspension bridge.

Follow the riverside path until you pass through a kissing-gate

60

and emerge into a very large pasture. Here the clear path bears right away from the river, crosses a wooden footbridge and heads towards a gate in the far wall. When you reach this, do not go through, but turn right along the nearside of the wall on a broad, grassy path. (Before you do this it is worth walking down to the river to look at the old stepping-stones, now only passable when the river is low, with Linton church beyond.)

When the wall turns left, keep forward, cross a small stream and bear left up the slope to a ladder-stile. Now bear slightly right, steeply up to another stile, then slightly left across a large field to a gated stile and signpost in the far wall, passing to the right of a stone barn and keeping to the right of the track leading from the barn up left to the farm. Shortly before you reach the stile you cross over another track. From the stile the next signpost is a short distance ahead. Here you will see that the path forks. Our goal is Hebden village, so we keep straight on to a ladder-stile to the left of a large gate.

The path is not high, but there are fine views, particularly to the moorland of the Barden Moor Access Area across the valley. Now we have a fence and old hedge to our right. Shortly before the end of the field the fence becomes a wall. Cross the stile, and now the wall is a fence again! In the far corner of this field cross the stile on the right and follow the wall on the left for a short distance to a stile in it. Cross this and the immediately-following footbridge and keep on, now with the wall again to your right.

Now the stiles are clear as you cross a succession of fields. After a time you pass through a gated stile. There is an old gateway immediately after it on the right, but no sign of the next stile. Follow the wall on your right along, but where it comes to a temporary end bear half-left across the field to a signpost on the other side, and now continue along with the wall to your left, but keep a close lookout for a gap-stile in it. Cross this and bear slightly right over a narrow field to a wall corner, then follow the wall down to the stile. The next stile is visible ahead. Now follow the wall on your right, pass through the gate in the corner, then keep forward to the gate which you will see at the far end of the next field (your direction is towards the church tower). Turn left along Hebden Back Lane, and when you reach the main road the pub is a few yards to the right.

⑬ Appletreewick
The Craven Arms

This peaceful Wharfedale village was a prosperous community in medieval times – mostly as a result of lead mining and sheep farming. Today, it attracts caravanners and walkers in search of peace and solitude among the hills and dales. Appletreewick's pretty name means 'dairy farm near an apple tree'.

The Craven Arms is a delightfully unspoilt, traditional village inn, a true gem among Britain's country pubs. Originally this 17th-century inn was part of the Craven Estate, built by Sir William Craven who was once Lord Mayor of London. For many years it was leased to local farmers who ensured their customers were given a warm welcome on market days! Inside, the cosy bar has much to catch the eye. Hoards of banknotes cover the beamed ceiling and a warming log fire in an iron range is a comforting sight in winter. Among the ales on hand-pump are Theakston XB, Best Bitter and Old Peculier, Tetley and Boddingtons. In summer there is usually a guest brew. Lagers include Heineken and Stella Artois. Strongbow and

Woodpecker cider are also on offer. Apart from the main bar, there is a snug and dining-room. Food is served every day and among the choices are various basket meals, ploughman's lunches, salads and sandwiches. There is a range of starters and more substantial meals include steak and kidney pie, fillet steak, deep fried haddock, lamb cutlets and mixed grill. Children are welcome, but no dogs please. Opening times are 11.30 am to 3 pm and 6.30 pm to 11 pm. Sunday hours are 12 noon to 3 pm and 7 pm to 10.30 pm.
Telephone: 01756 720270.

How to get there: Coming from the south, fork right off the B6160 Addingham to Burnsall road at Barden Tower and turn left at the next T-junction. From the north, Appletreewick is signposted off the B6265 Pateley Bridge to Grassington road.

Stone cottages in Appletreewick.

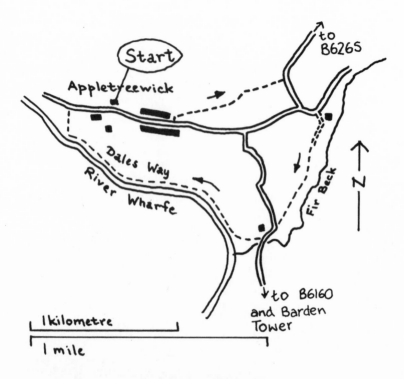

Parking: There is a car park at the inn.

Length of the walk: 3 miles. Map: OS Outdoor Leisure 10 Yorkshire Dales Southern area (inn GR 052601).

A typical Dales footpath making its way through a series of meadows and pastures by wall-stiles, and giving glorious views of Wharfedale, is followed by a gentle descent to the Wharfe and a return along the river bank.

The Walk

Leave the pub and turn left along the road through the village, noting some fine old houses, particularly Mock Beggar Hall and High Hall. Immediately after the church fork left up a cobbled drive which soon becomes tarmac and leads to a footpath sign. Bear right across the stile (in the direction of New Road). Now

64

the game of 'Who can spot the next stile?' begins! For the first few fields there is no problem, but then comes a point where the next field slopes down and no stile is visible. Head down, keeping close to the wall on your left, and the stile will be found in the bottom corner. Keep your direction over the next two fields, then bear slightly left across the corner of the following field. Now you can again see some of the stiles leading you through the walls ahead. The crag in the distance is Simon's Seat.

Having crossed the next stile, bear right along the wall on your right to the following one, then keep on from stile to stile until after climbing gently you again reach a point from where the next stile is invisible. Ahead of you, however, on the far side of the next wall there is a barn. Continue up the slope, heading well to the left of this barn, to reach a gated stile out onto a road. Ahead in the distance is the hamlet of High Skyreholme with the valley of Blands Beck.

Turn right down the road and follow it to the next junction, there turning sharp left along a 'No Through Road' (signposted 'Skyreholme'). Fork right off the road down the track to Howarth Farm, and at the farm buildings bear right with the track, which soon passes through a gate and reaches a caravan site. Where the track turns sharp left to the lower part of the site, keep straight on to a gated stile in the wall ahead.

Keep forward with the wall/fence to your left to the next stile. Fir Beck is down below on your left with the slopes of the Barden Fell Access Area beyond. Cross the stile and keep along the fence, but where this drops left downhill bear right along the top of the steep bank. When you draw level with a barn to your right, the path crosses a dip and regains the top of the bank. Now make for a modern bungalow in the dip ahead, but where a wall which you soon have on your right makes a sharp turn to the right, go with it to find a stile out onto a road.

Turn left down the road, but immediately before it crosses a bridge turn right off it through a gap in the wall (you are now on the Dales Way) and follow the clear path to the bank of the Wharfe, which here flows through a narrow gorge. There now follows a lovely section of riverside path. When you reach a fork, the left-hand branch leads in a few yards to a viewpoint overlooking rapids, the main path continuing to the right.

Follow the riverside path until, after a short section where it is enclosed, you have a wall to your right which soon turns sharp right away from the river and there is a signpost pointing back to Appletreewick. So leave the river, and follow the wall on an enclosed lane (there is a camp and caravan site on the left) which leads to a road. Turn right to return to your starting point, passing the fine old Low Hall on the way and noticing the ancient stocks just before you reach the pub.

14 Kirkby Malham
The Victoria Inn

Also known as the 'church place in Malhamdale', the stone village of Kirkby Malham lies close to the route of the Pennine Way, Britain's first long distance trail and officially opened in 1965, as well as the course of the meandering river Aire. The present church, which dates back to the late 15th century and is exceptionally large for such a small village, was built by the monks of Deerham Abbey, who owned the land. However, records indicate there has been a place of worship on this site for more than 1,000 years. The village may not be a sizeable community but the parish of Kirkby Malham extends for over 30 miles.

The Victoria Inn was built as a pub in 1840 and has long been the 'local' in this part of Malhamdale. A recent landlord was told by his customers when he first arrived there, 'just because you've bought it, doesn't mean to say it's yours!' During the summer it is open from 12 noon until 11 pm every day except Sunday, when the hours are 12 noon to 3 pm and 7 pm to

67

10.30 pm throughout the year. In winter the pub is open from 6 pm to 11 pm on Monday to Friday (closed at lunchtime) and 12 noon to 3 pm and 6 pm to 11 pm on Saturday. Real ales include Theakston Best Bitter and Old Peculier. There is usually a guest beer and a choice of several lagers is also on offer, as well as Guinness and Olde English cider. The dining-room has an à la carte menu. There is also a good range of bar food including soup of the day, prawn cocktail, liver and bacon, sirloin steak, beef in ale, beef curry, haddock and chips, scampi, salmon and spinach crêpe, pasta bake, vegetable casserole and cheese and onion flan. You will also find a children's menu and a daily specials board. Well-behaved dogs are welcome. Outside is a beer garden with a play area for children, and en suite accommodation is available for a longer stay.

Telephone: 01729 830213.

How to get there: From Skipton follow the A65 to Gargrave. Turn right towards Grassington, then follow the signs for Airton and Kirkby Malham. Cross the Kirkby Beck and the inn is on the left. From Settle take the A65 and turn left at Coniston Cold.

Parking: The inn has a car park. There is also room to park in the vicinity of the adjacent church.

Length of the walk: 2¾ miles. Map: OS Outdoor Leisure 10 Yorkshire Dales Southern area (inn GR 894609).

From the Victoria Inn the walk climbs above the village of Kirkby Malham and then heads for the outskirts of Airton. The final homeward leg is along the banks of the river Aire, following a section of the Pennine Way. A mile or so to the north is the famous beauty spot of Malham Cove, with its sheer limestone cliff rising more than 200 ft. It is said that the dark smuts on the cliff face – as if made by a chimney sweep – gave Charles Kingsley the inspiration for 'The Water Babies'.

The Walk

Leave the inn by turning right and walking towards the church. Just beyond the car park look for a waymarked path on the left – signposted to Otterburn. Follow the path over the pretty, tree-lined Kirkby Beck and then head up a flight of steps to a

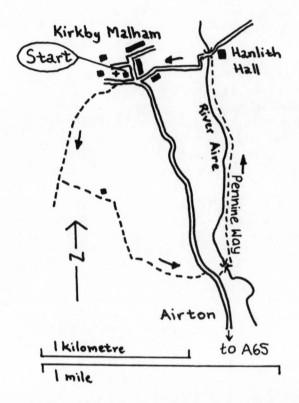

Kirkby Malham

Start

Hanlith Hall

River Aire

Pennine Way

N

Airton

1 Kilometre

to A65

1 mile

gate. Ascend the bank to a stile, then head on up the slope to the top boundary. There is an impressive view back to the rooftops of Kirkby Malham, dominated by the striking church tower of St Michael and All Angels. Keep going up the slope, with the fence and woodland on your immediate right. At the top cross a track to a stile. In the field veer left and cross this windswept high ground. Go down to a gill, cross the footbridge and head up the slope for a few yards to a gate and stile. Follow the field boundary until you come to a stepped stile on the left. There is a sign here for 'Airton – ½ mile'. Cross the stile and head across the grassy slopes.

Soon the corner of a wall comes into view. Make for the

corner and join a clear track, with the wall on the left. Make for a barn, pass through a gate and turn right at the sign. Cross a stile and then walk ahead across the pasture. Keep the wall close by you on the left and make for the far left corner of the field. In the next field continue along the boundary to the stile in the corner. Cross the enclosure to the next stile and then begin to veer left, still alongside the wall. Head for the apex of this enclosure, cross a stile, go down to a gate in the field corner, then follow the wall for a few yards until you reach a gap into the next field. Make for a gate in the next boundary, then cross the next field to its bottom right-hand corner, where a gate takes you out to the road.

Turn right and walk along the road for about 100 yards. Bear left at the sign for Malham and take the walled path down to the Aire. Cross the river and then swing left to join the route of the Pennine Way. Follow the path across the water-meadows and head towards a clump of trees and some gates.

Continue along the well-trodden river bank, pass an old dilapidated barn on the right, go through a wooden kissing-gate and keep on along the riverside path. Ahead is a graceful parkland landscape dotted with trees and from it are good views of Hanlith Hall. Eventually you come to a stone bridge over the Aire. Make for the stile and, on joining the road, turn left. Follow the lane back to the centre of Kirkby Malham and, at the crossroads, go straight over to the inn.

15 Long Preston
The Boar's Head

Long Preston, at the southern end of Ribblesdale, is a long, straggling village on the main Settle to Skipton road. Hard to believe but this community was once larger than the city of Leeds! Nearby is evidence of a Roman encampment, and Cromwell is reputed to have spent a night here.

The origins of the Boar's Head go back to the 18th century and inside the bar is an early black and white photograph depicting the inn in 1900. The first impression you get, as you pass through the entrance, is one of spaciousness and elbow-room. There is a bar, with tables and bench seats, a pool table, a games area and an adjoining dining-room. Tetley Bitter is on draught and there are several ciders, as well as Guinness, Kilkenny Irish beer, Carlsberg Export and Castlemaine XXXX. The bar menu lists home-made steak and kidney pie, fillet of fresh haddock, beef casserole in Guinness and scampi. Vegetable lasagne, gammon steak, rainbow trout, Scottish salmon, sirloin steak, Boars Head mixed grill, pasta and various vegetarian specialities are also on offer. The cold selection includes salad platters and freshly cut sandwiches. There is a choice of sweets, children's menu and a traditional Sunday roast. Families are welcome, as are well-behaved dogs. The inn is open from 11 am to 3 pm and 5 pm to midnight in winter. During the summer months (from Easter) the hours are 11 am to midnight. On Sunday throughout the year the pub is open from 12 noon to 3 pm and 7 pm to 10.30 pm. Overnight accommodation is also available.

Telephone: 01729 840217.

How to get there: Long Preston is on the A65 between Skipton and Settle. The village straddles the main road and the inn is on the left as you approach from the south.

Parking: The Boar's Head has its own car park.

Length of the walk: 2 ¾ miles. Map: OS Outdoor Leisure 10 Yorkshire Dales Southern area (inn GR 834581).

The walk leaves Long Preston and quickly heads for remote moorland where there are few signs of civilisation. Return to the village via various pastures and enclosures.

The Walk

Bear left on leaving the pub and walk along to the Maypole Inn. Turn right and follow the lane for a few yards. Take the first left turning into Green Gate Lane, which runs between walls. Pass several waymarked footpaths either side of you. Continue between trees and from here there are striking views back to the houses of Long Preston. Pass a footpath to the village on the left and keep going beside a copse on the right. Avoid the next turning (signposted 'Langber Lane') and continue to the next right-hand track which also leads eventually to Langber Lane.

Take the walled lane and head east between pastures. Further on, the lane bends left by a patch of woodland and descends to a footbridge. Cross the beck and then, faced with two ladder-stiles, take the right-hand one. Bear left and, with the wall on your left, head towards the next ladder-stile. Step across the beck at an appropriate spot and cross the field boundary.

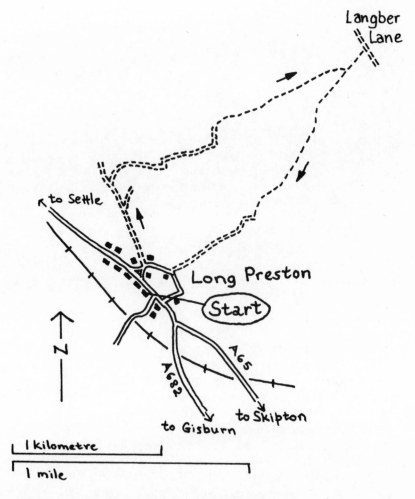

Langber Lane

to Settle

Long Preston

Start

N

A65

A682

to Gisburn

to Skipton

1 kilometre

1 mile

Continue now alongside the beck, following a rough path over lumpy ground and ragged, grassy slopes. The path gradually rises above the course of the beck and shortly you find yourself on the edge of open moorland. Continue in a north-easterly direction towards several gaps in the wall ahead. Make for the right-hand opening and follow the path into the next enclosure, keeping the dilapidated wall on your immediate left. Follow the edge of the pasture as far as its apex and here you will see a

73

Land of the Three Peaks. (John R Fawcett)

rough track running on to meet Langber Lane. At this point begin to head back to Long Preston by turning sharp right and following the left edge of the same field, now heading south-west. Look for a ladder-stile ahead and recross the boundary wall.

Head diagonally across the moorland expanse and make for the left-hand wall. Follow the line of the wall all the way down to a stepped stile in the corner. Continue ahead in the next pasture, keeping the wall on the left, cross another stile in the next boundary and maintain the same direction, with the wall on your right. Descend the bank and head for a footbridge to the left of the little reservoir. Cross the bridge (avoiding the path to Holme Bridge) and join a walled track, Scalehaw Lane. Follow it and soon the lane becomes metalled underfoot. Long Preston village and church edge into view along this stretch. At the next junction bear right, then follow the road round to the left. Pass the local school and at the green, by the Maypole Inn, turn left and walk back to the Boar's Head.

Stainforth
The Craven Heifer

16

More than 200 years ago packhorse traffic, on the route between Lancashire and the north-east, passed through the village of Stainforth and many of the traders would have called at the Craven Heifer. These travellers were probably the inn's first customers. Nearby is a famous packhorse bridge connecting the village with its neighbour Little Stainforth. The bridge, which spans the Ribble, is protected by the National Trust.

The Craven Heifer includes a no-smoking pool room, suitable for families, a taproom and dining-room. The main bar has panelled walls and a striking black and white photograph of the Ribblehead Viaduct. The inn is reputedly haunted by the ghost of a man who lived in the adjoining cottage. Thwaites Mild and Bitter are on handpump and there is a choice of lager – Carlsberg Export and Carling Black Label. Guinness and Strongbow draught cider are also available. The pub is famous in the area for its mixed grill, a noted speciality. Food is served

Stainforth Beck.

at every session and among the starters and bar snacks are home-made soup, small Yorkshire puddings, egg mayonnaise, ploughman's lunches and jacket potatoes. Some of the main courses are breaded haddock, steak and kidney pie and gammon, egg and pineapple. There is a range of vegetarian dishes, a choice of sandwiches and a children's menu. The restaurant menu includes various starters, vegetarian lasagne, venison medallions and cauliflower au gratin. On Sunday there is a traditional roast. In summer the pub is open from 11 am to 3 pm and 6 pm to 11 pm on Monday to Saturday. On Sunday the hours are 12 noon to 3 pm and 7 pm to 10.30 pm. During the winter months the inn is open from 12 noon to 2.30 pm and 6.30 pm to 11 pm on weekdays (closed Monday lunchtime) and from 11 am to 3 pm and 6.30 pm to 11 pm on Saturday. There is bed and breakfast accommodation and a beer garden. Children can play in the vicinity of the beck, which runs alongside the garden. No dogs please.

Telephone: 01729 822599.

How to get there: From Settle, just off the A65, take the B6479 northwards out of the town. Follow the signs for Stainforth and the inn is in the village centre, adjoining the bridge over the Stainforth Beck.

Parking: There is a small car park opposite the pub. If it is busy, use the public car park adjacent to the B6479.

Length of the walk: 3 miles. Map: OS Outdoor Leisure 2 Yorkshire Dales Western area (inn GR 822673).

There are frequent glimpses of the western Dales on this route, which traverses the high country north of Settle. Parts of the walk follow tracks once used by monks for sheep farming. A short detour takes you down to the spectacular Catrigg Force before beginning the return leg, which offers splendid views over the eastern slopes of Ribblesdale.

The Walk

From the inn turn left and cross the Stainforth Beck. When the road bends left go straight on for Halton Gill. Follow the lane round to the right and at this point you will probably catch a glimpse of some delightful stepping-stones crossing the beck. Further up is a signpost for 'Henside Road'. Take the track and follow it as it runs above the Stainforth Beck. Go through a gate and continue over a side beck. Once over it, bear left and head

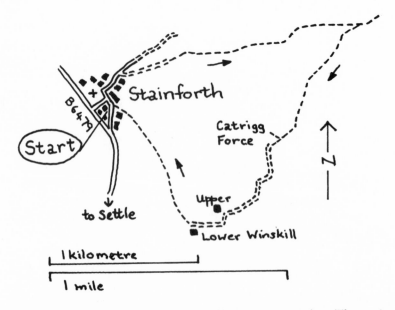

up the steep hillside, with a wall on your right. There is a glorious view from here across the rolling hills of Ribblesdale. Between the trees on the left are glimpses of a waterfall. Cross into the next field and then go straight on up to a ladder-stile in the next boundary. Continue straight ahead and at this stage of the walk there are views of Fountains Fell and Pen-y-ghent, their summits often covered by snow in winter.

Cross the pasture and, on reaching a wall, continue straight ahead, with the wall on your left. Make for another ladder-stile and keep alongside the wall. When it bends left veer half-right across the lonely moorland, making for the far corner of the pasture, where you should spot another ladder-stile. Cross the next pasture to yet another ladder-stile. Once over it bear right for a few steps to the next ladder-stile. Cross it and begin the homeward leg of this walk.

Head diagonally across this pasture and after a few minutes you will see a ladder-stile ahead of you in the boundary. Cross it and then follow the left-hand wall for about 50 yards. Cross a stile and turn right down the pasture. Look for a footbridge over the beck and then head for the far corner of this elongated enclosure. Cross a ladder-stile and walk along the edge of another pasture. Look for a sign for Henside Road and at this point cross the ladder-stile. Turn right and follow the boundary towards the next ladder-stile. There is a signposted path here leading down to Catrigg Force. Take the path and soon there are memorable views of the wooded gorge into which the highest waterfall in Ribblesdale plunges.

Return to the top track but do not bear right. Instead, take the cinder track up the slope to the next gate and ladder-stile. Cross the stile and then swing right towards Winskill. Follow the track as it cuts between walled pastures. Ahead of you are far-reaching views across a rumpled carpet of green hills and limestone dales. Follow the track down to a lane at High Winskill. Continue ahead for Stainforth. Walk down to the outbuildings of Lower Winskill. Go through a gate and continue ahead to a ladder-stile. Head up the bank and then bear right, following the yellow waymarker posts. As you cross the pasture you are treated to a breathtaking view of Ribblesdale. Stainforth and the B6479 road can be seen far below you. Cross another ladder-stile, then aim slightly left and walk alongside the craggy limestone edges which so perfectly characterise this part of the Dales. Head for another ladder-stile and then follow the path as it descends in somewhat slippery fashion between the trees.

The sound of traffic is audible now. Eventually you reach a kissing-gate at the foot of the wooded slopes. Maintain the same direction, keeping the woodland and fence on your right. Pass through a gate at the far end of the field, then walk diagonally down the next pasture and along a walled track to a stile. Bear left by some cottages to the road. Turn right, then immediately left and return to the inn.

17 Austwick
The Game Cock Inn

Austwick, one of the loveliest of all the Dales villages, acts as an excellent base for exploring the magnificent limestone hills of the western Dales. This is potholing country, where people descend into a dank, subterranean world of passages, caves and waterlogged caverns. The village is noted for its cottages and houses, some of which have elaborately carved lintels which indicate the names of previous owners and the date of the building.

The Game Cock Inn, which dates back to the early 17th century, has long been a famous hostelry in the area. Real ales on handpump include Thwaites Bitter, and you will also find Guinness, Strongbow draught cider and a choice of lagers – Carling Black Label, Carlsberg and Castlemaine XXXX. Starters or light meals range from soup and prawn cocktail to garlic mushrooms, jacket potatoes, sandwiches and toasties. For something more substantial you could choose deep fried plaice, scampi, battered haddock, steak and kidney pie, lasagne,

Cumberland sausage or maybe something from the grill. The children's menu includes beefburger, scampi and sausage. There is also a daily specials board. On Sunday a traditional roast is available. Food is served every day except on Monday, Tuesday and Wednesday evenings in winter and Monday evening in summer. The inn is open from 11.30 am to 2.30 pm and 6.30 pm to 11 pm on Monday to Saturday. On Sunday the hours are 12 noon to 3 pm and 7 pm to 10.30 pm. Children are welcome in the dining-room, verandah and garden. The Game Cock Inn also has two double and two single bedrooms. Telephone: 015242 51226.

How to get there: Austwick is just north of the A65 between Settle and Ingleton. The inn is on the left in the village centre, overlooking the green.

Parking: The Game Cock Inn has a small car park at the front.

Length of the walk: 4 miles. Map: OS Outdoor Leisure 2 Yorkshire Dales Western area (inn GR 766684).

Drystone walls in limestone country.

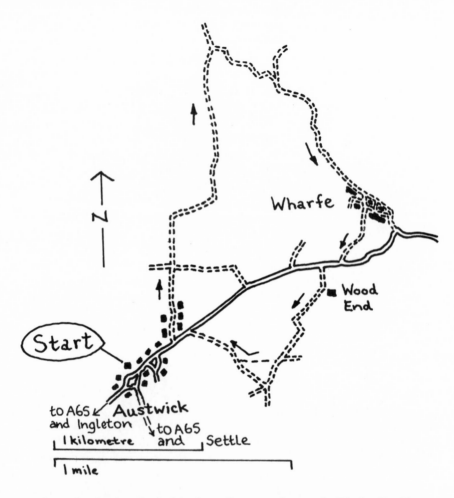

Wharfe

Wood
End

Start

to A65
and Ingleton

to A65
and Settle

Austwick

1 kilometre

1 mile

Soon after leaving Austwick, the walk passes close to the Norber Boulders, a famous geological feature in the land of the Three Peaks. This great limestone ridge is littered with huge boulders of dark Silurian slate. Further on, the route passes through the unspoilt hamlet of Wharfe, buried deep in the Dales and completely bypassed by through roads.

The Walk
From the inn turn left and walk along the village street, passing Orchard Leigh, a development of houses and bungalows. Pass the local school, then a stone cottage called Hobbs Gate. Turn

left into Town Head Lane and follow it as it winds between houses and cottages. The lane becomes progressively steeper as it begins to leave the village behind. Keep going as the lane ascends between trees and walls and gradually you will see wide vistas of endless, spacious landscapes opening up around you.

Pass a turning to Norber on the left and continue to follow the lane across this wild and primitive land of limestone edges and ancient boulders. The Norbers are known as 'erratics', meaning they do not naturally belong here. Towards the end of the last Ice Age these great boulders would have been carried here by the glacier that once occupied nearby Crummackdale.

Avoid public footpaths on either side and keep to the lane as it runs between walls. Further on, the lane becomes rougher and rutted underfoot. Eventually, you reach a track on the right (signposted 'Wharfe'). Take the bridleway and follow it down to a rather spectacular ford and clapper bridge, the waters of the Austwick Beck scurrying beneath you. Continue on the track and further on it narrows to a path, cutting between walls and sheltered banks of grass and bracken.

The path becomes sunken as it descends towards the charming little hamlet of Wharfe. Pass Garth Cottage and bear left at the junction. Avoid a turning on the left and continue on the main track as it cuts between fences and walls. At the road turn right and walk beside the Wharfe Gill Sike. Pass a footpath to Wood Lane and continue on the road until you reach a track on the left to Wood End Farm. Follow the track and when you reach the farmhouse swing right to join a walled track running between pastures and enclosures. Austwick can be seen in the distance.

The track bends sharp left at one point, then right. Pass a track running off sharp left and then just a few steps beyond the turning, with the path much narrower, bear right at a ladder-stile. Go diagonally across the field, passing close to the corner of a wall on the right. Head straight across to a ladder-stile in the next boundary. Cross the next pasture diagonally to reach another ladder-stile. Join a walled path and turn right. Take the clapper bridge across the Austwick Beck and make for the road. Bear left and return to the inn.

18 Chapel-le-Dale
The Old Hill Inn

Chapel-le-Dale is a lonely community nestling in the shadow of Ingleborough, one of the Three Peaks. The majestic hill, a favourite haunt of the legendary walker and author Alfred Wainwright, rises to 2,373 ft and dominates the rugged landscape in this part of the western Dales. The little church contains a tablet commemorating those men who perished whilst constructing the nearby Ribblehead Viaduct on the Settle/Carlisle railway in the 1870s.

The Old Hill Inn dates back to 1615 and was built to accommodate drovers transporting livestock between the Yorkshire Dales and Lancaster. Not surprisingly, these days the pub is especially popular with walkers and potholers. Even HRH the Prince of Wales has paid a visit to the inn, calling in to have a pint with the landlord whilst fulfilling an engagement in the area several years ago.

Food is served every day in the bar and dining-room and the pub is open from 11.30 am to 3 pm and 6.30 pm to 11 pm between Monday and Friday. On Saturday the hours are 11.30 am to 11 pm and on Sunday 12 noon to 3 pm and 7 pm to 10.30 pm. During the summer the inn is open all day on Friday. The bar is particularly quaint, with a roaring log fire in winter, stripped stone walls and beams. Among the ales on handpump are Dent Brewery Bitter, Castle Eden and Theakston Best and Old Peculier. Authentic Scrumpy cider is available, and a choice of European bottled beers. The menu includes a choice of starters – soup, black pudding and deep fried Camembert among them. Main courses range from roast beef, lasagne and chilli con carne to Old Peculier pie, scampi and lamb cutlets. There are light snacks, sandwiches, jacket potatoes and puddings. You will also find a specials board and on Sunday a traditional roast. There is a choice of sweets, and children have

Ribblehead viaduct. (Yorkshire and Humberside Tourist Board)

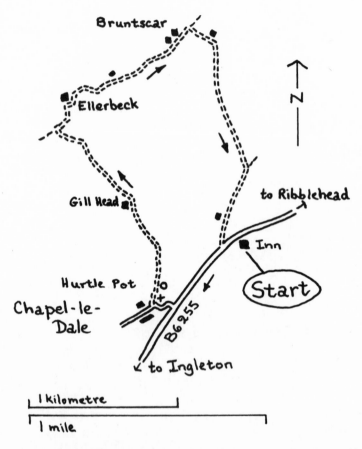

their own menu. The Old Hill Inn, which also offers two bunk rooms and three double rooms for overnight accommodation, welcomes dogs. It is probably wise to book if you want to eat in the dining-room.

Telephone: 015242 41256.

How to get there: The Old Hill Inn is on the B6255 road, between Ingleton and Hawes.

Parking: There is a spacious car park adjoining the pub.

Length of the walk: 3 miles. Map: OS Outdoor Leisure 2 Yorkshire Dales Western area (inn GR 743776).

From start to finish this walk follows tracks and minor roads with superb views over windswept hills and dales. Once or twice you are treated to glimpses of the magnificent Ribblehead Viaduct, a lasting tribute to the skill and expertise of the Victorian engineers who built it.

The Walk

Leave the inn by turning left and walk down the main road until you reach a turning for Chapel-le-Dale church on the right. Bear right and immediately pass the entrance to Nether Glen on the right. Pass St Leonard's church and then turn sharp right to join a lane running beneath some power cables and over a cattle grid. Avoid a track running off to the left to Middle Scales and High Scales and continue towards Gill Head and Ellerbeck. Climb between trees and lichen-covered boulders and soon you can see the outline of the Old Hill Inn. Continue on the track, pass over another cattle grid and stride out over open moorland pastures. In front of you now are the steeply rising slopes of West Fell. At the foot of the slopes are the buildings of Ellerbeck, the walk's next objective. Glancing to the right reveals a glimpse of Ribblehead Viaduct, its graceful arches blending perfectly with the dramatic Pennine landscape. At the next junction turn right for Ellerbeck. Follow the track between the outbuildings and on the right are magnificent views towards Ingleborough, its awesome bulk rising splendidly from a vast limestone plateau.

The track winds on to the buildings of Bruntscar. Beyond them, at the next junction, turn right for the Old Hill Inn. Follow the track alongside cattle sheds and milking parlours, cross a cattle grid and then head out over open pastures. Beyond another cattle grid you pass alongside a plantation. Cross several more cattle grids and then curve right, still following the lane, which has now graduated to tarmac. Follow it to the road and bear left. The Old Hill Inn is a short distance along the road.

⑲ Dent
The Sun Inn

With its quaint, whitewashed cottages and winding cobbled streets, Dent has long been a mecca for tourists and visitors. Today, the village economy relies mainly on farming and tourism but in the 17th and 18th centuries Dent echoed to the sound of clicking needles and spinning wheels. In those days daily village life revolved around this thriving cottage industry and stockings and gloves were produced in their thousands. Dent, the only village in Dentdale, has the highest main line railway station in England, located on the famous Settle/Carlisle line.

The Sun is a charming mid 17th-century inn with sturdy oak timbers and beams. Over the years it has been converted and enlarged. It also has its own brewery, which supplies Dent Bitter, Ramsbottom and T'Owd Tup to the inn. In addition, there is McEwan's lager, as well as Guinness and Dry Blackthorn cider. Among the dishes offered are cheeseburger and chips, home-made chicken curry, breaded haddock, Cumberland sausage, rump steak and vegetable lasagne. The cold table includes various sandwiches, salad and ploughman's lunches. Children's portions are also served. There is a daily specials board and a choice of sweets. During school holidays the inn is open between 11 am and 11 pm from Monday to Saturday. During term the hours are 11 am to 2.30 pm and 7 pm to 11 pm from Monday to Friday and all day on Saturday. On Sunday throughout the year the hours are 12 noon to 3 pm and 7 pm to 10.30 pm. Food is available every day. The Sun also has a pool room, a no-smoking area and bed and breakfast accommodation. Dogs are welcome in the bar.

Telephone: 01539 625326.

How to get there: Dent is signposted from Sedbergh, which is about 4 miles to the north-west. There is also a minor road from Ingleton in the south. From Hawes follow the B6255 towards Ingleton and then bear right for Cowgill and Dent.

Parking: The Sun has a car park at the rear of the inn. There is also a fee-paying public car park in Dent.

Length of the walk: 2 ¾ miles. Map: OS Outdoor Leisure 2 Yorkshire Dales Western area (inn GR 704869).

From Dent the walk heads for neighbouring Gawthrop and then returns to the village via the river Dee and a section of the Dales Way. Much of the route offers splendid views of Dentdale, one of the loveliest of all the Yorkshire Dales.

The Walk
From the inn turn left and walk along to the public car park. Bear left opposite the car park and follow the lane between houses. Pass The Old Vicarage on the right. When the lane bends left at the green, go straight ahead, following the bridleway towards Flinter Gill. Walk beside lines of pretty, whitewashed cottages and then after a few steps bear right at a wrought-iron kissing-gate (signposted 'Mill Beck'). There are good views over Dent on the right.

Follow the right-hand boundary of the field, cross into the next field and then make for the corner. Pass through a gated

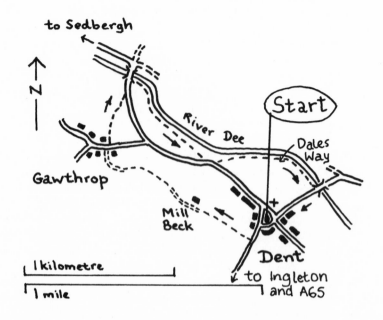

to Sedbergh

N

Start

River Dee

Dales Way

Gawthrop

Mill Beck

Dent

to Ingleton and A65

1 kilometre

1 mile

stile and go straight ahead across the field. Head down into the dip and soon you reach a pretty beck. Ahead of you are farm outbuildings. Cross the beck and then veer half-right. The scene is now dominated by a magnificent view of Dentdale. Aim for a galvanised farm gate and follow a concrete track between the outbuildings. Pass the cottages of Mill Beck and look for a sign for Gawthrop. Follow the track through several gates and then up the slope away from the buildings. Soon the track peters out and now you continue ahead across the field by maintaining the same direction. There are impressive views back towards Dent.

Look for a gateway in the dry-stone wall and go straight across to the gated stile in the next boundary. Continue ahead in the next field, with the boundary wall on your left. Aim for another stile and keep going towards some farm outbuildings. Join a firm track running alongside them and then pass some cottages. Follow the lane round to the right and at the junction, by some seats, bear right.

After a few yards begin to look for a signposted footpath on the left ('Barth Bridge'). Veer to the right of the house, pass through a gate and then take the waymarked path down the field edge. Oliver Gill runs beside you on the left. Pass through two gap-stiles with a wooded bank between them and then continue with the gill beside you, its waters scurrying beneath overhanging boughs and over rocky crags and boulders. Keep to the field edge and soon you will see the road ahead. Look for a gap in the boundary wall and pass into the adjacent field. Bear immediately right and walk along to the road.

Head towards Barth Bridge. However, before you cross the river Dee swing right to join the route of the Dales Way (signposted 'Hippins'). Cross the field, the Dee a short distance away, winding lazily through Dentdale. Continue across two field boundaries and beyond the second one, veer half-right to reach a double stile. Follow the river bank and soon the buildings of Dent come into view up ahead. Keep going to the road. Continue ahead towards Dent for a few moments, then swing obliquely left to rejoin the riverside path (signposted 'Church Bridge'). Follow the path beside the river and soon the bridge comes into view. Take the steps up to the road and turn right. Follow the road into Dent and pass the granite monument to Adam Sedgwick 1785 – 1873. Sedgwick was a famous pioneering geologist who never forgot his roots and often returned to Dent. Follow the lane round to the right and the inn is on the left.

⓴ Sedbergh
The Bull Hotel

With the Howgill Fells rising steeply behind it, Sedbergh's setting is perhaps more reminiscent of the Lake District than the Yorkshire Dales. This busy little town, acknowledged as the western gateway to the Dales, used to be in Yorkshire but was embraced by Cumbria as part of the 1974 county boundary changes. Sedbergh has strong Quaker links and the nearby meeting house dates back to 1675, thought to be the oldest of its kind in Northern England. For many years the main industries here focused on knitting and cotton spinning.

The Bull Hotel is a family-run hotel in the centre of Sedbergh. The bar is open from 11 am to 3 pm and 6 pm to 11 pm between Monday and Thursday, 11 am to 11 pm on Friday and Saturday and from 12 noon to 3 pm and 7 pm to 10.30 pm on Sunday. Food is served every day. Beers drawn from the pump include Trophy, Marston's Pedigree and Boddingtons. There are usually several guest ales. Also available are Woodpecker and Strongbow ciders, Guinness, and Heineken and Stella Artois

lagers. The bar and dining-room menu includes a wide selection of dishes. Among the starters are home-made soup, crispy mushrooms, platter of prawns and farmhouse-style pâté. There are various toasted sandwiches, home-made hot platters – including steak pie, chicken curry and braised liver and onions – vegetarian dishes, a choice of grills and steaks and a range of fish dishes. There are also several salads and ploughman's lunches and a daily specials board. On Sunday a traditional roast is served. Booking is a good idea at weekends. Both families and dogs are welcome. The Bull Hotel also has a beer garden.
Telephone: 01539 620264.

How to get there: Sedbergh is on the A684, about 6 miles to the east of junction 37 of the M6. The inn is in Main Street.

Parking: There is room to park at the rear of the Bull Hotel and a public car park further along Main Street.

Length of the walk: 3¼ miles. Map: OS Outdoor Leisure 2 Yorkshire Dales Western area (inn GR 657923).

Sedbergh.

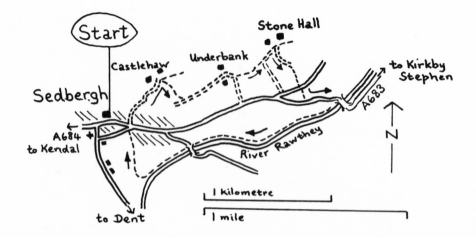

Map labels: Start, Stone Hall, Castlehaw, Underbank, Sedbergh, A684, to Kendal, to Kirkby Stephen, A683, River Rawthey, N, 1 kilometre, 1 mile, to Dent

On leaving Sedbergh the walk passes close to the site of a Norman motte-and-bailey castle before making for the banks of the river Rawthey.

The Walk

From the inn turn left and walk along the cobbled street. Pass the National Westminster Bank on the left and head down to the road junction. Bear left towards Castlehaw. Go up the track between houses and soon it curves right to run up between lines of trees and dry-stone walls, leaving the buildings of Sedbergh behind it. On the higher ground you break cover from the trees and continue on the track as it cuts between pastures and grassy enclosures. Swing left at the farm buildings, following the waymarker. Cross the beck and then bear immediately right. Follow the level path with the beck down below you on the right. After several moments make for a gap-stile on the right. Head down the slope and into the trees of a copse. Pass through the trees, cross another beck and then a stile before skirting the field edge. The beck is just below you on the right and a short distance beyond it is the perimeter of Castlehaw, a Norman motte-and-bailey castle constructed to defend Garsdale and the Rawthey valley, both of which can be seen at this stage of the walk. The path graduates to a track and

94

runs down to a lane. Go through a wrought-iron kissing-gate and turn left towards Underbank. Pass some bungalows and continue along the lane between hedgerows. There are constant, dramatic views over grassy hillsides and sweeping fells, creating a spectacular picture.

Pass between stone cottages – one of which is Underbank – and then follow the waymarker. The drive curves to the right and cuts between stone pillars. Follow it as it goes across open fields. As the drive bends sharp right, go straight ahead over a stile into the field. Cross it, veering slightly left as you approach the far boundary. Cross the footbridge and walk ahead, with the boundary wall on your immediate right. In the field corner go out to a lane and bear left. Avoid a track veering off half-left towards Ghyll Farm and head for a cattle grid. Note the montana clematis in the garden on your left. Once over the cattle grid turn right, pass through a gate and then walk ahead along a grassy track. The boundary wall is on your right. Head down the right-hand edge of the field and ahead of you are glorious views over Garsdale and distant fells. Soon the track curves to the left in line with a row of bushes. Further down you come to a stile by a beck. Cross it and then make for a stile on the far side of the beck, easily fordable at this stage. Cross the stile, bear right and walk down the field, with the water now on your right. Cross the lane and continue ahead towards the A683.

Make for the stone stile and go out to the road. Turn left and follow the roadside verge. Pass a farm and, beyond a layby, look for a waymarked path on the right. Take the path down to the river bank. Follow the path back towards Sedbergh, keeping the river Rawthey down below you on the left. Soon you reach the confluence of the Rawthey and the Clough river and here there are glimpses of spectacular falls and rapids. Continue to a ladder-stile and then walk ahead across the watermeadows to a footbridge over a side beck. The river is wide here, lined by trees and shingle banks. Keep going, passing various field boundaries and soon the houses of Sedbergh loom into view.

In due course you come alongside a dry-stone wall. The path runs between the wall and river. Make for some steps and go up to the road. Turn right for several steps and then rejoin the riverside path (signposted 'Winder House'). Pass through a kissing-gate and begin to look for a stile on the right. Cross it and then bear left along a path enclosed by trees and a wall. Go diagonally right in the next field to another stile. Veer slightly left as you ascend the steep slope and make for a gap-stile in the top boundary. Follow the right-hand boundary of the next field and head down to a wrought-iron kissing-gate in the corner. There are excellent views from here over the rooftops of Sedbergh.

Go straight on at the entrance to Winder House, still keeping to the boundary. Join a drive and follow it into Sedbergh. At the next junction cross over into Main Street and return to the inn.